The Poetry of John Bunyan

Volume III (of III)

John Bunyan was born in 1628. His fame emanates from the allegorical book The Pilgrim's Progress. A classic of the English language.

A committed non-conformist Bunyan's life covered two seminal periods in English history: The English Civil War and the Restoration of Charles II. He fought in the former and was subject to over 12 years in prison during the latter.

Whilst this caused great hardship, even more so one expects to his young wife and their children, his spirit and determination to remain dutifully worshipping of his faith was undoubted and resolute.

It is with particular pleasure that we bring you perhaps a side to his life that has not been fully appreciated. His poetry. Across their verses and number are works of quite remarkable thought.

John Bunyan died in 1688, just short of his 60th birthday and is buried in Bunhill Fields in London.

Index of Contents

ONE THING IS NEEDFUL;

or, SERIOUS MEDITATIONS UPON THE FOUR LAST THINGS: DEATH, JUDGMENT, HEAVEN, AND HELL UNTO WHICH IS ADDED EBAL AND GERIZZIM, OR THE BLESSING AND THE CURSE,

ADVERTISEMENT BY THE EDITOR

According to Charles Doe, in that curious sheet called The Struggler for the Preservation of Mr. John Bunyan's Labours, these poems were published about the year 1664, while the author was suffering imprisonment for conscience sake, very probably in separate sheets or tracts, to be sold by his wife or children, to aid in their humble maintenance. They were afterwards united to form a neat little volume, 32 mo. The editor is the fortunate possessor of the third edition, being the last that was printed during the author's lifetime, and with his latest corrections. From this the present edition has been accurately reprinted. The three tracts are distinct as to pages; a strong indication that they were originally separate little volumes. A copy of the fourth edition of this extremely rare book, without date, and somewhat larger in size, is in the British Museum, in which the pages are continued throughout the volume.

These poems are upon subjects the most solemn and affecting to all mankind, and, like all Bunyan's other works, were evidently written, not for display, but to impress upon the heart those searching realities upon which depend our everlasting destiny. Die we must; yes, reader, you and I must follow our fathers to the unseen world. Heaven forbid that we should be such mad fools, as to make no provision for the journey; no inquiries about our prospects in that eternity into which we must so soon enter. True it is, that unless Heaven stops us in our mad career, we shall plunge into irretrievable ruin.

In the first of these poems, many of the minute circumstances attendant on death are pressed upon the memory. Very soon, as Bunyan awfully expresses the though, we must look death in the face, and 'drink with him.' Soon some kind friend or relative will close our eyelids, and shut up our glassy eyes for ever; tie up the fallen jaw, and prepare the corrupting body for its long, but not final resting-place. Our hour-glass is fast ebbing out; time stands ready with his scythe to cut us down; the grave yawns to receive us. 'Man dieth and wasteth away; yea, man giveth up the ghost, and where is he' (Job 14:10). The answer is ready, sure, certain—he goes to the judgment of the great day. There every thought that has passed over his mind, while on earth, will be manifested and scrutinized; every action, every sin, and every supposed good work, however private, will then be published. It is an awful thought. Thousands of works which are thought good will be weighed in the unerring balances of truth, will be found wanting, and proved to be bad, not arising from evangelical motives; while all our thoughts, words, and actions will appear in their real colours tainted by sin. Those only who are clothed in the Redeemer's righteousness, and cleansed by his purifying, sanctifying sufferings, can stand accepted, and will receive the invitation, Come, ye blessed, inherit the kingdom of your father, and your God, by adoption into his family; while an innumerable multitude will be hurried away by the voice of the judge, Go, ye cursed, into everlasting torment. Solemn consideration. Reader, have you fled for refuge to the hope set before you in the gospel? Have you felt the alarm in your soul under a sense of sin and judgment? Were you dead, and are you made alive? O, then, while you bless the Saviour for such unspeakable mercies, seek with all diligence, as life is prolonged, to extend the blessing to others. There is no work nor device in the grave, whither we are all hastening, that can benefit mortals. The great gulf will be fixed, and our state be finally decided for eternity. O, then, if you have not yet attained that good hope of heavenly felicity, sure and stedfast—hasten—yes,

'Hasten, O sinner, to be blest
And stay not for the morrow's sun;
For fear the curse should thee arrest
Before the morrow be begun.'

GEO. OFFOR.

ONE THING IS NEEDFUL,

OR

AN INTRODUCTION TO THE ENSUING DISCOURSE.

I
These lines I at this time present
To all that will them heed,
Wherein I show to what intent
God saith, Convert[2] with speed.

II
For these four things come on apace,
Which we should know full well,
Both death and judgment, and, in place
Next to them, heaven and hell.

III
For doubtless man was never born
For this life and no more:
No, in the resurrection morn
They must have weal or woe.

IV
Can any think that God should take
That pains, to form a man
So like himself, only to make
Him here a moment stand?

V
Or that he should make such ado,
By justice, and by grace;
By prophets and apostles too,
That men might see his face?

VI
Or that the promise he hath made,
Also the threatenings great,
Should in a moment end and fade?
O! no, this is a cheat.

VII
Besides, who is so mad, or worse,
To think that Christ should come
From glory, to be made a curse,
And that in sinners' room,

VIII
If nothing should by us be had
When we are gone from hence,
But vanities, while here? O mad
And foolish confidence.

IX
Again, shall God, who is the truth,
Say there is heaven and hell
And shall men play that trick of youth
To say, But who can tell?

X
Shall he that keeps his promise sure
In things both low and small,
Yet break it like a man impure,
In matters great'st of all?

XI
O, let all tremble at that thought,
That puts on God the lie,
That saith men shall turn unto nought
When they be sick and die.

XII
Alas, death is but as the door
Through which all men do pass,
To that which they for evermore
Shall have by wrath or grace.

XIII
Let all therefore that read my lines,
Apply them to the heart:
Yea, let them read, and turn betimes,
And get the better part.

XIV
Mind therefore what I treat on here,
Yea, mind and weigh it well;
'Tis death and judgment, and a clear
Discourse of heaven and hell.

OF DEATH

Death, as a king rampant and stout
The world he dare engage;
He conquers all, yea, and doth rout
The great, strong, wise, and sage.

No king so great, nor prince so strong,
But death can make to yield,
Yea, bind and lay them all along,
And make them quit the field.

Where are the victors of the world,
With all their men of might?
Those that together kingdoms hurl'd,
By death are put to flight.

How feeble is the strongest hand,
When death begins to gripe!
The giant now leaves off to stand,
Much less withstand and fight.

The man that hath a lion's face
Must here give place and bend,
Yea, though his bones were bars of brass,
'Tis vain here to contend.

Submit he must to feeble ones,
To worms who will enclose
His skin and flesh, sinews and bones,
And will thereof dispose

Among themselves, as merchants do
The prizes they have got;
Or as the soldiers give unto
Each man the share and lot,

Which they by dint of sword have won,
From their most daring foe;
While he lies by as still as stone,
Not knowing what they do.

Beauty death turns to rottenness,
And youth to wrinkled face;
The witty he brings to distress,
And wantons to disgrace.

The wild he tames, and spoils the mirth
Of all that wanton are,
He takes the worldling from his worth,
And poor man from his care.

Death favours none, he lays at all,
Of all sorts and degree;
Both old and young, both great and small,
Rich, poor, and bound, and free.

No fawning words will flatter him,
Nor threat'nings make him start;
He favours none for worth or kin,
All must taste of his dart.

What shall I say? the graves declare

That death shall conquer all;
There lie the skulls, dust, bones, and there
The mighty daily fall.

The very looks of death are grim
And ghastly to behold;
Yea, though but in a dead man's skin,
When he is gone and cold.

How 'fraid are some of dead men's beds,
And others of their bones;
They neither care to see their heads,
Nor yet to hear their groans.

Now all these things are but the shade
And badges of his coat;[3]
The glass that runs, the scythe and spade,
Though weapons more remote:

Yet such as make poor mortals shrink
And fear, when they are told,
These things are signs that they must drink
With death; O then how cold.

It strikes them to the heart! how do
They study it to shun!
Indeed who can bear up, and who
Can from these shakings run?

But how much more then when he comes
To grapple with thy heart;
To bind with thread thy toes and thumbs,[4]
And fetch thee in his cart?

Then will he cut thy silver cord,
And break thy golden bowl;
Yea, break that pitcher which the Lord
Made cabin for thy soul.

Thine eyes, that now are quick of sight,
Shall then no way espy
How to escape this doleful plight,
For death will make thee die.

Those legs that now can nimbly run,
Shall then with faintness fail
To take one step, death's dart to shun,
When he doth thee assail.

That tongue that now can boast and brag
Shall then by death be tied

So fast, as not to speak or wag,
Though death lies by thy side.

Thou that didst once incline thine ear
Unto the song and tale,
Shall only now death's message hear,
While he, with face most pale,

Doth reason with thee how thy days
Hath hitherto been spent;
And what have been thy deeds and ways,
Since God thee time hath lent

Then will he so begin to tear
Thy body from thy soul,
And both from life, if now thy care
Be not on grace to roll.

Death puts on things another face
Than we in health do see:
Sin, Satan, hell, death, life and grace
Now great and weighty be.

Yea, now the sick man's eye is set
Upon a world to come:
He also knows too without let[5]
That there must be his home.

Either in joy, in bliss and light,
Or sorrow, woe, and grief;
Either with Christ and saints in white,
Or fiends, without relief.

But, O! the sad estate that then
They will be in that die
Both void of grace and life! poor men!
How will they fear and cry.

Ha! live I may not, though I would
For life give more than all;
And die I dare not, though I should
The world gain by my fall.

No, here he must no longer stay,
He feels his life run out,
His night is come, also the day
That makes him fear and doubt.

He feels his very vitals die,
All waxeth pale and wan;
Nay, worse, he fears to misery

He shortly must be gone.

Death doth already strike his heart
With his most fearful sting
Of guilt, which makes his conscience start,
And quake at every thing.

Yea, as his body doth decay
By a contagious grief,
So his poor soul doth faint away
Without hope or relief.

Thus while the man is in this scare,
Death doth still at him lay;
Live, die, sink, swim, fall foul or fair,[6]
Death still holds on his way.

Still pulling of him from his place,
Full sore against his mind;
Death like a sprite stares in his face,
And doth with links him bind.

And carries him into his den,
In darkness there to lie,
Among the swarms of wicked men
In grief eternally.

For only he that God doth fear
Will now be counted wise:
Yea, he that feareth him while here,
He only wins the prize.

'Tis he that shall by angels be
Attended to that bliss
That angels have; for he, O he,
Of glory shall not miss.

Those weapons and those instruments
Of death, that others fright:
Those dreadful fears and discontents
That brings on some that night.

That never more shall have a day,
Brings this man to that rest
Which none can win but only they
Whom God hath called and blest

With the first fruits of saving grace,
With faith, hope, love, and fear
Him to offend; this man his face
In visions high and clear,

Shall in that light which no eye can
Approach unto, behold
The rays and beams of glory, and
Find there his name enroll'd,

Among those glittering starts of light
That Christ still holdeth fast
In his right hand with all his might,
Until that danger's past,

That shakes the world, and most hath dropt
Into grief and distress,
O blessed then is he that's wrapt
In Christ his righteousness.

This is the man death cannot kill,
For he hath put on arms;
Him sin nor Satan hath not skill
To hurt with all their charms.

A helmet on his head doth stand,
A breastplate on his heart:
A shield also is in his hand,
That blunteth every dart.

Truth girds him round the reins, also
His sword is on his thigh;
His feet in shoes of peace do go
The ways of purity.

His heart it groaneth to the Lord,
Who hears him at his call,
And doth him help and strength afford,
Wherewith he conquers all.

Thus fortified, he keeps the field
While death is gone and fled;
And then lies down upon his shield
Till Christ doth raise the dead.

OF JUDGMENT

As 'tis appointed men should die,
So judgment is the next
That meets them most assuredly;
For so saith holy text.

Wherefore of judgment I shall now

Inform you what I may,
That you may see what 'tis, and how
'Twill be with men that day.

This world it hath a time to stand,
Which time when ended, then
Will issue judgment out of hand
Upon all sorts of men.

The Judge we find, in God's record,
The Son of man, for he
By God's appointment is made Lord
And Judge of all that be.

Wherefore this Son of man shall come
At last to count with all,
And unto them shall give just doom,
Whether they stand or fall.

Behold ye now the majesty
And state that shall attend
This Lord, this Judge, and Justice high
When he doth now descend.

He comes with head as white as snow,
With eyes like flames of fire;
In justice clad from top to toe,
Most glorious in attire.

His face is filled with gravity;
His tongue is like a sword;
His presence awes both stout and high,
The world shakes at his word.

He comes in flaming fire, and
With angels clear and bright,
Each with a trumpet in his hand,
Clothed in shining white.

The trump of God sounds in the air,
The dead do hear his voice;
The living too run here and there,
Who made not him their choice.

Thus to his place he doth repair,
Appointed for his throne,
Where he will sit to judge, and where
He'll count with every one.

Angels attending on his hand
By thousands on a row;

Yea, thousand thousands by him stand,
And at his beck do go.

Thus being set, the books do ope
In which all crimes are writ.
All virtues, too, of faith and hope,
Of love; and every whit

Of all that man hath done or said,
Or did intend to do;
Whether they sinn'd, or were afraid
Evil to come into.

Before this bar each sinner now
In person must appear;
Under his judgment there to bow
With trembling and with fear:

Within whose breast a witness then
Will certainly arise,
That to each charge will say Amen,
While they seek and devise

To shun the sentence which the Lord
Against them then will read,
Out of the books of God's record,
With majesty and dread.

But every heart shall opened be
Before this judge most high;
Yea, every thought to judgment he
Will bring assuredly.

And every word and action, too,
He there will manifest;
Yea, all that ever thou didst do,
Or keep within thy breast,

Shall then be seen and laid before
The world, that then will stand
To see thy judge open ev'ry sore,
And all thy evils scann'd.

Weighing each sin and wickedness
With so much equity,
Proportioning of thy distress
And woful misery.

With so much justice, doing right,
That thou thyself shalt say,
My sins have brought me to this plight,

I threw myself away.

Into that gulph my sins have brought
Me justly to possess,
For which I blame not Christ, I wrought
It out by wickedness.

But O! how willingly would these
That thus in judgment be,
If that they might have help or ease,
Unto the mountains flee.

They would rejoice if that they might
But underneath them creep,
To hide them from revenging right,
For fear of which they weep.

But all in vain, the mountains then
Will all be fled and gone;
No shelter will be found for men
That now are left alone.

For succour they did not regard
When Christ by grace did call
To them, therefore they are not heard,
No mountains on them fall.

Before this Judge no one shall shroud
Himself, under pretence
Of knowledge, which hath made him proud,
Nor seeming penitence.

No high profession here can stand,
Unless sincerity
Hath been therewith commixed, and
Brought forth simplicity.[7]

No mask nor vizor here can hide
The heart that rotten is;
All cloaks now must be laid aside,
No sinner must have bliss.

Though most approve of thee, and count
Thee upright in thy heart;
Yea, though preferred and made surmount
Most men to act thy part,

In treading where the godly trod,
As to an outward show;
Yet this hold still, the grace of God
Takes hold on but a few,

So as to make them truly such
As then shall stand before
This Judge with gladness; this is much
Yet true for evermore.

The tree of life this paradise
Doth always beautify,
'Cause of our health it is the rise
And perpetuity.

Here stands the golden throne of grace
From out of which do run
Those crystal streams that make this place
Far brighter than the sun.

Here stands mount Zion with her king.
Jerusalem above,
That holy and delightful thing,
So beautified with love.

That, as a mother succours those
Which of her body be,
So she far more, all such as close
In with her Lord; and she

Her grace, her everlasting doors
Will open wide unto
Them all, with welcome, welcome, poor,
Rich, bond, free, high and low,

Unto the kingdom which our Lord
Appointed hath for all
That hath his name and word ador'd;
Because he did them call

Unto that work, which also they
Sincerely did fulfil,
Not shunning always to obey
His gracious holy will.

Besides, this much doth beautify
This goodly paradise,
That from all quarters, constantly,
Whole thousands as the price

Of precious blood, do here arrive;
As safe escaping all,
Sin, hell, and satan did contrive
To bring them into thrall.

Each telling his deliverance
I' th' open face of heaven;
Still calling to remembrance
How fiercely they were driven

By deadly foe, who did pursue
As swift as eagles fly;
Which if thou have not, down thou must
With those that then shall die
The second death, and be accurs'd
Of God. For certainly,

The truth of grace shall only here
Without a blush be bold
To stand, whilst others quake and fear,
And dare not once behold.

That heart that here was right for God
Shall there be comforted;
But those that evil ways have trod,
Shall then hang down the head.

As sore confounded with the guilt
That now upon them lies,
Because they did delight in filth
And beastly vanities.

Or else because they did deceive
With hypocritical
Disguises, their own souls, and leave
Or shun that best of all

Approved word of righteousness,
They were invited to
Embrace, therefore they no access
Now to him have, but woe.

For every one must now receive
According to their ways;
They that unto the Lord did cleave,
The everlasting joys.

Those that did die in wickedness,
To execution sent,
There still to grapple with distress,
Which nothing can prevent.

Of which two states I next shall write,
Wherefore I pray give ear,
And to them bend with all our might
Your heart with filial fear.

OF HEAVEN

Heaven is a place, also a state,
It doth all things excel,
No man can fully it relate,
Nor of its glory tell.

God made it for his residence,
To sit on as a throne,
Which shows to us the excellence
Whereby it may be known.

Doubtless the fabric that was built
For this so great a king,
Must needs surprise thee, if thou wilt
But duly mind the thing.

If all that build do build to suit
The glory of their state,
What orator, though most acute,
Can fully heaven relate?

If palaces that princes build,
Which yet are made of clay,
Do so amaze when much beheld,
Of heaven what shall we say?

It is the high and holy place;
No moth can there annoy,
Nor make to fade that goodly grace
That saints shall there enjoy.

Mansions for glory and for rest
Do there prepared stand;
Buildings eternal for the blest
Are there provided, and

The glory and the comeliness
By deepest thought none may
With heart or mouth fully express,
Nor can before that day.

These heav'ns we see, be as a scroll,
Or garment folded up,
Before they do together roll,
And we call'd in to sup.

There with the king, the bridegroom, and

By him are led into
His palace chambers, there to stand
With his prospect to our view.

And taste and smell, and be inflam'd,
And ravished to see
The buildings he hath for us fram'd,
How full of heaven they be.

Its state also is marvellous,
For beauty to behold;
All goodness there is plenteous,
And better far than gold,

Adorn'd with grace and righteousness,
While fragrant scents of love
O'erflow with everlasting bliss,
All that do dwell above.

The heavenly majesty, whose face
Doth far exceed the sun,
Will there cast forth its rays of grace
After this world is done.

Which rays and beams will so possess
All things that there shall dwell,
With so much glory, light, and bliss,
That none can think or tell.

That wisdom which doth order all
Shall there be fully shown;
That strength that bears the world there shall
By every one be known.

That holiness and sanctity
Which doth all thought surpass,
Shall there in present purity
Outshine the crystal glass.

The beauty and the comeliness
Of this Almighty shall
Make amiable with lasting bliss
Those he thereto shall call.

The presence of this God will be
Eternal life in all,
And health and gladness, while we see
Thy face, O immortal!

Here will the Lord make clear and plain
How sweetly did agree

His attributes, when Christ was slain
Our Saviour to be.

How wisdom did find out the way,
How strength did make him stand,
How holiness did bear the sway,
And answer just demand.

How all these attributes did bend
Themselves to work our life,
Through the Christ whom God did send
To save us by his might.

All this will sparkle in our eye
Within the holy place,
And greatly raise our melody,
And flow our hearts with grace.

The largest thought that can arise
Within the widest heart
Shall then be filled with surprize,
And pleas'd in every part.

All mysteries shall here be seen,
And every knot, unty'd;
Electing love, that hid hath been,
Shall shine on every side.

The God of glory here will be
The life of every one;
Whose goodly attributes shall we
Possess them as our own.

By wisdom we all things shall know,
By light all things shall see,
By strength, too, all things we shall do,
When we in glory be.

The Holy Lamb of God, also,
Who for our sakes did die,
The holy ones of God shall know,
And that most perfectly.

Those small and short discoveries
That we have of him here,
Will there be seen with open eyes,
In visions full and clear.

Those many thousand acts of grace
That here we feel and find,
Shall there be real with open face

Upon his heart most kind.

There he will show us how he was
Our prophet, priest, and king;
And how he did maintain our cause,
And us to glory bring.

There we shall see how he was touch'd
With all our grief and pain
(As in his word he hath avouch'd),
When we with him shall reign;

He'll show us, also, how he did
Maintain our faith and love,
And why his face sometimes he hid
From us, who are his dove;

These tempting times that here we have,
We there shall see were good;
Also that hidden strength he gave,
The purchase of his blood.

That he should stand for us before
His Father, thus we read.
But then shall see, and shall adore
Him for his gracious deed.

Though we are vile, he without shame
Before the angels all
Lays out his strength, his worth, and name,
For us, who are in thrall.

This is he who was mock'd and beat,
Spit on, and crown'd with thorns;
Who for us had a bloody sweat,
Whose heart was broke with scorns.

'Tis he who stands so much our friend,
As shortly we shall see,
With open face, world without end,
And in his presence be.

That head that once was crown'd with thorns,
Shall now with glory shine;
That heart that broken was with scorns,
Shall flow with life divine;

That man that here met with disgrace,
We there shall see so bright;
That angels can't behold his face
For its exceeding light.

What gladness will possess our heart
When we shall see these things!
What light and life, in every part,
Will rise like lasting springs!

O blessed face and holy grace,
When shall we see this day?
Lord, fetch us to this goodly place
We humbly do thee pray.

Next to this Lamb we shall behold
All saints, both more and less,
With whit'ned robes in glory roll'd,
'Cause him they did confess.

Each walking in his righteousness
With shining crowns of gold,
Triumphing still in heav'nly bliss,
Amazing to behold.

Each person for his majesty
Doth represent a king;
Yea, angel-like for dignity,
And seraphims that sing.

Each motion of their mind, and so
Each twinkling of their eye;
Each word they speak, and step they go,
It is in purity.

Immortal are they every one,
Wrapt up in health and light,
Mortality from them is gone,
Weakness is turn'd to might.

The stars are not so clear as they,
They equalize the sun;
Their glory shines to perfect day,
Which day will ne'er be done.

No sorrow can them now annoy,
Nor weakness, grief or pain;
No faintness can abate their joy,
They now in life do reign.

They shall not there, as here, be vex'd
With Satan, men, or sin;
Nor with their wicked hearts perplex'd,
The heavens have cop'd[8] them in.

Thus, as they shine in their estate,
So, too, in their degree;
Which is most goodly to relate,
And ravishing to see.

The majesty whom they adore,
Doth them in wisdom place
Upon the thrones, and that before
The angels, to their grace.

The saints of the Old Testament,
Full right to their degree;
Likewise the New, in excellent
Magnificency be.

Each one his badge of glory wears,
According to his place;
According as was his affairs
Here, in the time of grace.

Some on the right hand of the Lamb,
Likewise some on the left,
With robes and golden chains do stand
Most grave, most sage, and deft.[9]

The martyr here is known from him
Who peaceably did die,
Both by the place he sitteth in,
And by his dignity.

Each father, saint, and prophet shall,
According to his worth,
Enjoy the honour of his call,
And plainly hold it forth.

Those bodies which sometimes were torn,
And bones that broken were
For God's word; he doth now adorn
With health and glory fair.

Thus, when in heav'nly harmony
These blessed saints appear,
Adorn'd with grace and majesty,
What gladness will be there!

The light, and grace, and countenance,
The least of these shall have,
Will so with terror them advance,
And make their face so grave,

That at them all the world will shake,

When they lift up their head;
Princes and kings will at them quake,
And fall before them dead.

This shall we see, thus shall we be,
O would the day were come,
Lord Jesus take us up to thee,
To this desired home.

Angels also we shall behold,
When we on high ascend,
Each shining like to men of gold,
And on the Lord attend.

These goodly creatures, full of grace,
Shall stand about the throne,
Each one with lightning in his face,
And shall to us be known.

These cherubims with one accord
Shall cry continually,
Ah, holy, holy, holy, Lord,
And heavenly majesty.

These will us in their arms embrace,
And welcome us to rest,
And joy to see us clad with grace,
And of the heavens possess'd.

This we shall hear, this we shall see,
While raptures take us up,
When we with blessed Jesus be,
And at his table sup.

Oh shining angels! what, must we
With you lift up our voice?
We must; and with you ever be,
And with you must rejoice.

Our friends that lived godly here,
Shall there be found again;
The wife, the child, and father dear,
With others of our train.

Each one down to the foot in white,
Fill'd to the brim with grace,
Walking among the saints in light,
With glad and joyful face.

Those God did use us to convert,
We there with joy shall meet,

And jointly shall, with all our heart,
In life each other greet.

A crown to them we then shall be,
A glory and a joy;
And that before the Lord, when he
The world comes to destroy.

This is the place, this is the state,
Of all that fear the Lord;
Which men nor angels may relate
With tongue, or pen, or word.

No night is here, for to eclipse
Its spangling rays so bright;
Nor doubt, nor fear to shut the lips,
Of those within this light.

The strings of music here are tun'd
For heavenly harmony,
And every spirit here perfum'd
With perfect sanctity.

Here runs the crystal streams of life,
Quite through all our veins.
And here by love we do unite
With glory's golden chains.

Now that which sweet'neth all will be
The lasting of this state;
This heightens all we hear or see
To a transcendant rate.

For should the saints enjoy all this
But for a certain time,
O, how would they their mark then miss,
And at this thing repine?

Yea, 'tis not possible that they
Who then shall dwell on high,
Should be content, unless they may
Dwell there eternally.

A thought of parting with this place
Would bitter all their sweet,
And darkness put upon the face
Of all they there do meet.

But far from this the saints shall be,
Their portion is the Lord,
Whose face for ever they shall see,

As saith the holy word.

And that with everlasting peace,
Joy, and felicity,
From this time forth they shall increase
Unto eternity.

OF HELL, AND THE ESTATE OF THOSE THAT PERISH

Thus, having show'd you what I see
Of heaven, I now will tell
You also, after search, what be
The damned wights of hell.

And O, that they who read my lines
Would ponder soberly,
And lay to heart such things betimes
As touch eternity.

The sleepy sinner little thinks
What sorrows will abound
Within him, when upon the brinks
Of Tophet he is found.

Hell is beyond all though a state
So doubtful[10] and forlorn,
So fearful, that none can relate
The pangs that there are born.

God will exclude them utterly
From his most blessed face,
And them involve in misery,
In shame, and in disgrace.

God is the fountain of all bliss,
Of life, of light, and peace;
They then must needs be comfortless
Who are depriv'd of these.

Instead of life, a living death
Will there in all be found.
Dyings will be in every breath,
Thus sorrow will abound.

No light, but darkness here doth dwell;
No peace, but horror strange:
The fearful damning wights[11] of hell
In all will make this change.

To many things the damned's woe
Is liked in the word,
And that because no one can show
The vengeance of the Lord.

Unto a dreadful burning lake,
All on a fiery flame,
Hell is compared, for to make
All understand the same.

A burning lake, a furnace hot,
A burning oven, too,
Must be the portion, share, and lot,
Of those which evil sow.

This plainly shows the burning heat
With which it will oppress
All hearts, and will like burnings eat
Their souls with sore distress.

This burning lake, it is God's wrath
Incensed by the sin
Of those who do reject his path,
And wicked ways walk in.

Which wrath will so perplex all parts
Of body and of soul,
As if up to the very hearts
In burnings they did roll.

Again, to show the stinking state
Of this so sad a case,
Like burning brimstone God doth make
The hidings of his face.

And truly as the steam, and smoke,
And flames of brimstone smell,
To blind the eyes, and stomach choke,
So are the pangs of hell.

To see a sea of brimstone burn,
Who would it not affright?
But they whom God to hell doth turn
Are in most woful plight.

This burning cannot quenched be,
No, not with tears of blood;
No mournful groans in misery
Will here do any good.

O damned men! this is your fate,

The day of grace is done,
Repentance now doth come too late,
Mercy is fled and gone.

Your groans and cries they sooner should
Have sounded in mine ears,
If grace you would have had, or would
Have me regard your tears.

Me you offended with your sin,
Instructions you did slight,
Your sins against my law hath been,
Justice shall have his right.

I gave my Son to do you good,
I gave you space and time
With him to close, which you withstood,
And did with hell combine.

Justice against you now is set,
Which you cannot appease;
Eternal justice doth you let
From either life or ease.

Thus he that to this place doth come
May groan, and sigh, and weep;
But sin hath made that place his home,
And there it will him keep.

Wherefore, hell in another place
Is call'd a prison too,
And all to show the evil case
Of all sin doth undo.

Which prison, with its locks and bars
Of God's lasting decree,
Will hold them fast; O how this mars
All thought of being free!

Out at these brazen bars they may
The saints in glory see;
But this will not their grief allay,
But to them torment be.

Thus they in this infernal cave
Will now be holden fast
From heavenly freedom, though they crave,
Of it they may not taste.

The chains that darkness on them hangs
Still ratt'ling in their ears,

Creates within them heavy pangs,
And still augments their fears.

Thus hopeless of all remedy,
They dyingly do sink
Into the jaws of misery,
And seas of sorrow drink.

For being cop'd[12] on every side
With helplessness and grief,
Headlong into despair they slide
Bereft of all relief.

Therefore this hell is called a pit,
Prepared for those that die
The second death, a term most fit
To show their misery.

A pit that's bottomless is this,
A gulf of grief and woe,
A dungeon which they cannot miss,
That will themselves undo.

Thus without stay they always sink,
Thus fainting still they fail,
Despair they up like water drink,
These prisoners have no bail.

Here meets them now that worm that gnaws,
And plucks their bowels out,
The pit, too, on them shuts her jaws;
This dreadful is, no doubt.

This ghastly worm is guilt for sin,
Which on the conscience feeds,
With vipers' teeth, both sharp and keen,
Whereat it sorely bleeds.

This worm is fed by memory,
Which strictly brings to mind,
All things done in prosperity,
As we in Scripture find.

No word, nor thought, nor act they did,
But now is set in sight,
Not one of them can now be hid,
Memory gives them light.

On which the understanding still
Will judge, and sentence pass,
This kills the mind, and wounds the will,

Alas, alas, alas!

O, conscience is the slaughter shop,
There hangs the axe and knife,
'Tis there the worm makes all things hot,
And wearies out the life.

Here, then, is execution done
On body and on soul;
For conscience will be brib'd of none,
But gives to all their dole.

This worm, 'tis said, shall never die,
But in the belly be
Of all that in the flames shall lie,
O dreadful sight to see!

This worm now needs must in them live,
For sin will still be there,
And guilt, for God will not forgive,
Nor Christ their burden bear.

But take from them all help and stay,
And leave them to despair,
Which feeds upon them night and day,
This is the damned's share.

Now will confusion so possess
These monuments of ire,
And so confound them with distress,
And trouble their desire.

That what to think, or what to do,
Or where to lay their head,
They know not; 'tis the damned's woe
To live, and yet be dead.

These cast-aways would fain have life,
But know, they never shall,
They would forget their dreadful plight,
But that sticks fast'st of all.

God, Christ, and heaven, they know are best,
Yet dare not on them think,
The saints they know in joys do rest,
While they their tears do drink.

They cry alas, but all in vain,
They stick fast in the mire,
They would be rid of present pain,
Yet set themselves on fire.

Darkness is their perplexity,
Yet do they hate the light,
They always see their misery,
Yet are themselves all night.

They are all dead, yet live they do,
Yet neither live nor die.
They die to weal, and live to woe,
This is their misery.

Amidst all this so great a scare
That here I do relate,
Another falleth to their share
In this their sad estate.

The legions of infernal fiends
Then with them needs must be,
A just reward for all their pains,
This they shall feel and see.

With yellings, howlings, shrieks, and cries,
And other doleful noise,
With trembling hearts and failing eyes,
These are their hellish joys.

These angels black they would obey,
And serve with greedy mind,
And take delight to go astray,
That pleasure they might find.

Which pleasure now like poison turns
Their joy to heaviness;
Yea, like the gall of asps it burns,
And doth them sore oppress

Now is the joy they lived in
All turned to brinish tears,
And resolute attempts to sin
Turn'd into hellish fears.

The floods run trickling down their face,
Their hearts do prick and ache,
While they lament their woful case,
Their loins totter and shake.

O wetted cheeks, with bleared eyes,
How fully do you show
The pangs that in their bosom lies,
And grief they undergo!

Their dolour in their bitterness
So greatly they bemoan,
That hell itself this to express
Doth echo with their groan.

Thus broiling on the burning grates,
They now to wailing go,
And say of those unhappy fates
That did them thus undo.

Alas, my grief! hard hap had I
Those dolours here to find,
A living death, in hell I lie,
Involv'd with grief of mind.

I once was fair for light and grace,
My days were long and good;
I lived in a blessed place
Where was most heav'nly food.

But wretch I am, I slighted life,
I chose in death to live;
O, for these days now, if I might,
Ten thousand worlds would give.

What time had I to pray and read,
What time to hear the word!
What means to help me at my need,
Did God to me afford!

Examples, too, of piety
I every day did see,
But they abuse and slight did I,
O, woe be unto me.

I now remember how my friend
Reproved me of vice,
And bid me mind my latter end,
Both once, and twice, and thrice.

But O, deluded man, I did
My back upon him turn;
Eternal life I did not heed,
For which I now do mourn.

Ah, golden time, I did thee spend
In sin and idleness,
Ah, health and wealth, I did you lend
To bring me to distress.

My feet to evil I let run,

And tongue of folly talk;
My eyes to vanity hath gone,
Thus did I vainly walk.

I did as greatly toil and strain
Myself with sin to please,
As if that everlasting grain
Could have been found in these.

But nothing, nothing have I found
But weeping, and alas,
And sorrow, which doth now surround
Me, and augment my cross.

Ah, bleeding conscience, how did I
Thee check when thou didst tell
Me of my faults, for which I lie
Dead while I live in hell.

I took thee for some peevish foe,
When thou didst me accuse,
Therefore I did thee buffet so,
And counsel did refuse.

Thou often didst me tidings bring,
How God did me dislike,
Because I took delight in sin,
But I thy news did slight.

Ah, Mind, why didst thou do those things
That now do work my woe?
Ah, Will, why was thou thus inclin'd
Me ever to undo?

My senses, how were you beguil'd
When you said sin was good?
It hath in all parts me defil'd,
And drown'd me like a flood.

Ah, that I now a being have,
In sorrow and in pain;
Mother, would you had been my grave,
But this I wish in vain.

Had I been made a cockatrice,
A toad, or such-like thing;[13]
Yea, had I been made snow or ice,
Then had I had no sin;

A block, a stock, a stone, or clot,
Is happier than I;

For they know neither cold nor hot,
To live nor yet to die.

I envy now the happiness
Of those that are in light,
I hate the very name of bliss,
'Cause I have there no right.

I grieve to see that others are
In glory, life, and well,
Without all fear, or dread, or care,
While I am racked in hell.

Thus will these souls with watery eyes,
And hacking of their teeth,
With wringing hands, and fearful cries,
Expostulate their grief.

O set their teeth they will, and gnash,
And gnaw for very pain,
While as with scorpions God doth lash
Them for their life so vain.

Again, still as they in this muse,
Are feeding on the fire,
To mind there comes yet other news,
To screw their torments higher.

Which is the length of this estate,
Where they at present lie;
Which in a word I thus relate,
'Tis to eternity.

This thought now is so firmly fix'd
In all that comes to mind,
And also is so strongly mix'd
With wrath of every kind.

So that whatever they do know,
Or see, or think, or feel,
For ever still doth strike them through
As with a bar of steel.

For EVER shineth in the fire,
EVER is on the chains;
'Tis also in the pit of ire,
And tastes in all their pains.

For ever separate from God,
From peace, and life, and rest;
For ever underneath the rod

That vengeance liketh best.

O ever, ever, this will drown'd
Them quite and make them cry,
We never shall get o'er thy bound,
O, great eternity!

They sooner now the stars may count
Than lose these dismal bands;
Or see to what the motes[14] among
Or number up the sands.

Then see an end of this their woe,
Which now for sin they have;
O wantons, take heed what you do,
Sin will you never save.

They sooner may drink up the sea,
Than shake off these their fears;
Or make another in one day
As big with brinish tears;

Than put an end to misery,
In which they now do roar,
Or help themselves; no, they must cry,
Alas, for evermore.

When years by thousands on a heap
Are passed o'er their head;
Yet still the fruits of sin they reap
Among the ghostly dead.

Yea, when they have time out of mind
Be in this case so ill,
For EVER, EVER is behind[15]
Yet for them to fulfill.

EBAL AND GERIZZIM,

OR THE BLESSING AND THE CURSE:

BEING A SHORT EXHORTATION TO SINNERS, BY THE MERCY AND SEVERITY OF GOD.

FROM MOUNT GERIZZIM

Besides what I said of the Four Last Things,
And of the weal and woe that from them springs;
An after-word still runneth in my mind,
Which I shall here expose unto that wind

That may it blow into that very hand
That needs it. Also that it may be scann'd
With greatest soberness, shall be my prayer,
As well as diligence and godly care;
So to present it unto public view,
That only truth and peace may thence ensue.

My talk shall be of that amazing love
Of God we read of; which, that it may prove,
By its engaging arguments to save
Thee, I shall lay out that poor help I have
Thee to entice; that thou wouldst dearly fall
In love with thy salvation, and with all
That doth thereto concur, that thou mayst be
As blessed as the Blessed can make thee,
Not only here but in the world to come,
In bliss, which, I pray God, may be thy home.

But first, I would advise thee to bethink
Thyself, how sin hath laid thee at the brink
Of hell, where thou art lulled fast asleep
In Satan's arms, who also will thee keep
As senseless and secure as e'er he may,
Lest thou shouldst wake, and see't, and run away
Unto that Jesus, whom the Father sent
Into the world, for this cause and intent,
That such as thou, from such a thrall as this
Might'st be released, and made heir of bliss.
Now that thou may'st awake, the danger fly,
And so escape the death that others die,
Come, let me set my trumpet to thine ear,
Be willing all my message for to hear:
'Tis for thy life, O do it not refuse;
Wo unto them good counsel do abuse.
Thou art at present in that very case,
Which argues thou art destitute of grace:
For he that lies where sin hath laid him, lies
Under the curse, graceless, and so he dies
In body and in soul, within that range,
If God his heart in mercy doth not change
Before he goes the way of all the earth,
Before he lose his spirit and his breath,
Repentance there is none within the grave,
Nor Christ, nor grace, nor mercies for to save
Thee from the vengeance due unto thy sin,
If now thou dost not truly close with him.

Thou art like him that sleepeth in the sea
On broken boards, which, without guide or stay,
Are driven whither winds and water will;
While greedy beasts do wait to have their fill

By feeding on his carcass, when he shall
Turn overboard, and without mercy fall
Into the jaws of such as make a prey
Of those whom justice drowneth in the sea.

Thou art like him that snoring still doth lie
Upon the bed of vain security,
Whilst all about him into burning flame
By fire is turned; yea, and while the frame
And building where he lies consuming is,
And while himself these burnings cannot miss.

Thou art like one that hangeth by a thread
Over the mouth of hell, as one half-dead;
And O, how soon this thread may broken be,
Or cut by death, is yet unknown to thee!
But sure it is, if all the weight of sin,
And all that Satan, too, hath doing been,
Or yet can do, can break this crazy thread,
'Twill not be long before, among the dead,
Thou tumble do, as linked fast in chains,
With them to wait in fear for future pains.

What shall I say? Wilt thou not yet awake?
Nor yet of thy poor soul some pity take?
Among the lions it hood-winked lies;
O, that the Lord would open once thine eyes
That thou might'st see it, then I dare say thou,
As half-bereft of wits, wouldst cry out, How
Shall I escape? Lord help, O! help with speed,
Reach down thy hand from heav'n, for help I need,
To save me from the lions, for I fear
This soul of mine they will in pieces tear.

Come, then, and let us both expostulate
The case betwixt us, till we animate
And kindle in our hearts that burning love
To Christ, to grace, to life, that we may move
Swifter than eagles to this blessed prey;
Then shall it be well with us in that day
The trump shall sound, the dead made rise, and stand,
Then to receive, for breach of God's command,
Such thunder-claps as these, Depart from me
Into hell-fire, you that the wicked be,
Prepared for the devil, and for those
That with him and his angels rather chose
To live in filthy sin and wickedness,
Whose fruit is everlasting bitterness.

We both are yet on this side of the grave,
We also gospel-privileges have;

The word, and time to pray; God give us hearts,
That, like the wise man, we may act our parts,
To get the pearl of price; then we shall be
Like godly Mary, Peter, Paul, and we
Like Jacob, too, the blessing shall obtain;
While Esau rides a-hunting for the gain
Of worldly pelf, which will him not avail
When death or judgment shall him sore assail.

Now, to encourage us for to begin,
Let us believe the kingdom we may win,
And be possess'd thereof, if we the way
Shall hit into, and then let nothing stay
Or hinder us; the crown is at the end,
Let's run and strive, and fly, and let's contend
With greatest courage it for to obtain;
'Tis life, and peace, and everlasting gain.
The gate of life, the new and living way,
The promise holdeth open all the day,
Which thou by Jacob's ladder must ascend,
Where angels always wait, and do attend
As ministers, to minister for those
That do with God, and Christ, and glory close.

If guilt of sin still lieth at our door,
Us to discourage, let us set before
Our eyes a bleeding Jesus, who did die
The death, and let's believe the reason why
He did it, was that we might ever be
From death and sin, from hell and wrath set free.
Yea, let's remember for that very end
It was his blessed Father did him send;
That he the law of God might here fulfil,
That so the mystery of his blessed will
Might be revealed in the blessedness
Of those that fly to Christ for righteousness.

Now let us argue with ourselves, then, thus
That Jesus Christ our Lord came to save us,
By bearing of our sins upon his back,
By hanging on the cross as on a rack,
While justice cut him off on every side,
While smiles Divine themselves from him did hide,
While earth did quake, and rocks in pieces rent,
And while the sun, as veiled, did lament
To see the innocent and harmless die
So sore a death, so full of misery.

Yea, let us turn again, and say, All this
He did and suffered for love of his.
He brought in everlasting righteousness,

That he might cover all our nakedness;
He wept and wash'd his face with brinish tears
That we might saved be from hellish fears;
Blood was his sweat, too, in his agony,
That we might live in joyful ecstasy;
He apprehended was and led away,
That grace to us-ward never might decay.
With swords, and bills, and outrage in the night,
That to the peace of heav'n we might have right.
Condemned he was between two thieves to die,
That we might ever in his bosom lie;
Scourged with whips his precious body were,
That we lashes of conscience might not fear;
His head was crowned with thorns, that we might be
Crowned with glory and felicity;
He hanged was upon a cursed tree,
That we delivered from death might be;
His Father from him hides his smiles and face,
That we might have them in the heavenly place;
He cry'd, My God, why hast forsaken me?
That we forsaken of him might not be.
Into his side was thrust a bloody spear,
That we the sting of death might never fear;
He went into the grave after all this,
That we might up to heav'n go, and have bliss.
Yea, rise again he did out of the earth,
And shook off from him all the chains of death;
Then at his chariot wheels he captive led
His foes, and trod upon the serpent's head;
Riding in triumph to his Father's throne,
There to possess the kingdom as his own.
What say'st thou, wilt not yet unto him come?
His arms are open, in his heart is room
To lay thee; be not then discouraged,
Although thy sins be many, great, and red;
Unto thee righteousness he will impute,
And with the kisses of his mouth salute
Thy drooping soul, and will it so uphold,
As that thy shaking conscience shall be bold
To come to mercy's seat with great access,
There to expostulate with that justice
That burns like fiery flames against all those
That do not with this blessed Jesus close;
Which unto thee will do no harm, but good,
Because thou hast reliance on that blood
That justice saith hath given him content,
For all that do unfeignedly repent
Their ill-spent life, and roll upon free grace,
That they within that bosom might have place,
That open is to such, where they shall lie
In ease, and gladness, and felicity,

World without end, according to that state
I have, nay, better than I, can relate.

If thou shalt still object, thou yet art vile,
And hast a heart that will not reconcile
Unto the holy law, but will rebel,
Hark yet to what I shall thee farther tell.
Two things are yet behind that help thee will,
If God should put into thy mind that skill,
So to improve them as becometh those
That would with mercy and forgiveness close.
 First, then, let this sink down into thy heart,
That Christ is not a Saviour in part,
But every way so fully he is made
That all of those that underneath his shade
And wing would sit, and shroud their weary soul,
That even Moses dare it not control,
But justify it, approve of 't, and conclude
No man nor angel must himself intrude
With such doctrine that may oppose the same,
On pain of blaspheming that holy name,
Which God himself hath given unto men,
To stay, to trust, to lean themselves on, when
They feel themselves assaulted, and made fear
Their sin will not let them in life appear.

For as God made him perfect righteousness,
That he his love might to the height express,
And us present complete before the throne;
Sanctification, too, of his own
He hath prepared, in which do we stand,
Complete in holiness, at his right hand.
Now this sanctification is not
That holiness which is in us, but that
Which in the person of this Jesus is,
And can inherently be only his.
But is imputed to us for our good.
As is his active righteousness and blood;
Which is the cause, though we infirm are found,
That mercy and forgiveness doth abound
To us-ward, and that why we are not shent[16]
And empty, and away rebuked sent,
Because that all we do imperfect is.
Bless God, then, for this holiness of his,
And learn to look by faith on that alone,
When thou seest thou hast nothing of thine own;
Yea, when thy heart most willing is to do
What God by his good word doth call thee to;
And when thou find'st most holiness within,
And greatest power over every sin,
Yet then to Jesus look, and thou shalt see

In him sanctification for thee,
Far more complete than all that thou canst find
In the most upright heart and willing mind,
That ever man or angels did possess,
When most filled with inherent righteousness.
Besides, if thou forgettest here to live,
And Satan get thee once into his sieve,
He will so hide thy wheat, and show thy brun[17]
That thou wilt quickly cry, I am undone.
Alas, thy goodliest attainments here,
Though like the fairest blossoms they appear,
How quickly will they lour and decay,
And he as if they all were fled away,
When once the east-wind of temptations beat
Upon thee, with their dry and blasting heat!
Rich men will not account their treasure lies
In crack'd groats and four-pence half-pennies,[18]
But in those bags they have within their chests,
In staple goods, which shall within their breasts
Have place accordingly, because they see
Their substance lieth here. But if that be
But shaken, then they quickly fear, and cry,
Alas, 'tis not this small and odd money,
We carry in our pockets for to spend,
Will make us rich, or much will stand our friend.
If famine or if want do us assail,
How quickly will these little pieces fail!

If thou be wise, consider what I say
And look for all in Christ, where no decay
Is like to be; then though thy present frame
Be much in up-and-down, yet he the same
Abideth, yea, and still at God's right hand,
As thy most perfect holiness will stand.
It is, I say, not like to that in thee,
Now high, then low, now out, then in, but he
Most perfect is, when thou art at the worst
The same, the very same; I said at first,
This helpeth much when thou art buffeted,
And when thy graces lie in thee as dead;
Then to believe they are all perfect still
In Christ thy head, who hath that blessed skill,
Yet to present thee by what is in him
Unto his Father, one that hath no sin.
Yea, this will fill thy mouth with argument
Against the tempter, when he shall present
Before thee all thy weakness, and shall hide
From thee thy graces, that thou mayst abide
Under the fretting fumes of unbelief,
Which never yielded Christian man relief.
Nor help thyself thou mayst against him thus:

O Satan, though my heart indeed be worse
Than 'twas a while ago, yet I perceive
Thou shalt me not of happiness bereave,
Nor yet of holiness; for by the Word
I find that Jesus Christ, our blessed Lord,
Is made sanctification for me
In his own person, where all graces be,
As water in the fountain; and that I,
By means of that, have yet a sanctity,
Both personal and perfect every way;
And that is Christ himself, as Paul doth say.
Now, though my crazy pitcher oft doth leak,
By means of which my graces are so weak,
And so much spent, that one I cannot find
Able to stay or help my feeble mind;
Yet then I look to Jesus, and see all
In him that wanting is in me, and shall
Again take courage, and believe he will
Present me upright in his person, till
He humble me for all my foolishness,
And then again fill me with holiness.
Now, if thou lovest inward sanctity,
As all the saints do most unfeignedly,
Then add, to what I have already said,
Faith in the promise; and be not afraid
To urge it often at the throne of grace,
And to expect it in its time and place.
Then he that true is, and that cannot lie,
Will give it unto thee, that thou thereby
Mayst serve with faith, with fear, in truth and love,
That God that did at first thy spirit move
To ask it to his praise, that he might be
Thy God, and that he might delight in thee.

If I should here particulars relate,
Methinks it could not but much animate
Thy heart, though very listless to inquire
How thou mayst that enjoy, which all desire
That love themselves and future happiness;
But O, I cannot fully it express:
The promise is so open and so free,
In all respects, to those that humble be,
That want they cannot what for them is good;
But there 'tis, and confirmed is with blood,
A certain sign, all those enjoy it may,
That see they want it, and sincerely pray
To God the Father, in that Jesus' name
Who bled on purpose to confirm the same.

[THE NECESSITY OF A NEW HEART.]

Now wouldst thou have a heart that tender is,
A heart that forward is to close with bliss;
A heart that will impressions freely take
Of the new covenant, and that will make
The best improvement of the word of grace,
And that to wickedness will not give place;
All this is in the promise, and it may
Obtained be of them that humbly pray.
Wouldst thou enjoy that spirit that is free,
And looseth those that in their spirits be
Oppressed with guilt, or filth, or unbelief;
That spirit that will, where it dwells, be chief;
Which breaketh Samson's cord as rotten thread,
And raiseth up the spirit that is dead;
That sets the will at liberty to choose
Those things that God hath promis'd to infuse
Into the humble heart? All this, I say,
The promise holdeth out to them that pray.

[THE SPIRIT OF PRAYER.]

Wouldst thou have that good, that blessed mind,
That is so much to heavenly things inclin'd
That it aloft will soar, and always be
Contemplating on blest eternity.
That mind that never thinks itself at rest,
But when it knows it is for ever blest;
That mind that can be here no more content,
Than he that in the prison doth lament;
That blessed mind that counts itself then free
When it can at the throne with Jesus be,
There to behold the mansions he prepares
For such as be with him and his co-heirs.
This mind is in the covenant of grace,
And shall be theirs that truly seek his face.

[OF GODLY FEAR.]

Is godly fear delightful unto thee,
That fear that God himself delights to see
Bear sway in them that love him? then he will
Thy godly mind in this request fulfil.
By giving thee a fear that tremble shall,
At every trip thou takest, lest thou fall,
And him offend, or hurt thyself by sin,
Or cause poor souls that always blind have been
To stumble at thy falls, and harder be
Against their own salvation and thee.

That fear that of itself would rather choose
The rod, than to offend or to abuse

In anything that blessed worthy name,
That hath thee saved from that death and shame;
That sin would soon have brought thee to, if he
Had not imputed righteousness to thee.
I will love them, saith God, and not depart
From them, but put my fear within their heart,
That I to them may always lovely be,
And that they never may depart from me.

[OF UPRIGHTNESS AND SINCERITY.]

Wouldst thou be very upright and sincere?
Wouldst thou be that within thou dost appear,
Or seem to be in outward exercise
Before the most devout, and godly wise?
Yea, art thou thus when no eye doth thee see
But that which is invisible? and be
The words of God in truth thy prop and stay?
And do they in thy conscience bear more sway
To govern thee in faith and holiness,
Than thou canst with thy heart and mouth express?
And do the things that truly are divine,
Before thee more than gold or rubies shine?
And if, as unto Solomon, God should
Propound to thee, What wouldst thou have? how would
Thy heart and pulse beat after heav'nly things,
After the upper and the nether springs?

Couldst, with unfeigned heart and upright lip,
Cry, Hold me fast, Lord, never let me slip,
Nor step aside from faith and holiness,
Nor from the blessed hope of future bliss?
Lord, rather cross me anywhere than here;
Lord, fill me always with thy holy fear,
And godly jealousy of mine own heart,
Lest I, Lord, should at any time depart
From thy most blessed covenant of grace,
Where Jesus rules as King, and where thy face
Is only to be seen with comfort, and
Where sinners justified before thee stand.

If these thy groanings be sincere and true,
If God doth count thee one that dost pursue
The things thou cryest after with thy heart,
No doubt but in them thou shalt have a part.

[HOW GRACES ARE TO BE OBTAINED.]

The next word that I would unto thee say,
Is how thou mayst attain without delay,
Those blessed graces, and that holiness

Thou dost with so much godly zeal express
Thy love to, and thy longing to enjoy,
That sins and weakness might thee less annoy.
Know, then, as I have hinted heretofore,
And shall now speak unto a little more,
All graces in the person of the Son
Are by the Father hid, and therefore none
Can them obtain but they who with him close;
All others graceless are but only those;
For of his fulness 'tis that we receive,
And grace for grace; let no man then deceive
Himself or others with a feigned show
Of holiness, if Jesus they eschew.
When he ascended to his Father, then
It was that he received gifts for men;
Faith, hope, and love, true zeal, an upright heart,
Right humbleness of mind, and every part
Of what the word of life counts holiness,
God then laid up in him, that we redress
And help might have, who do unto him fly
For righteousness and gospel sanctity.

[OF IMPUTED RIGHTEOUSNESS.]

Now, if thou wouldst inherit righteousness,
And so sanctification possess
In body, soul, and spirit, then thou must
To Jesus fly, as one ungodly first;
And so by him crave pardon for thy sin
Which thou hast loved, and hast lived in;
For this cannot at all forgiven be,
For any righteousness that is in thee;
Because the best thou hast is filthy rags,
Profane, presumptuous, and most beastly brags
Of flesh and blood, which always cross doth lie
To God, to grace, and thy felicity.

Then righteousness imputed thou must have,
Thee from that guilt and punishment to save
Thou liest under as a sinful man,
Throughout polluted, and that never can
By any other means acquitted be,
Or ever have true holiness in thee.
The reason is, because all graces are
Only in Christ, and be infused where,
Or into those whom he doth justify,
By what himself hath done, that he thereby
Might be the whole of all that happiness
The sinner shall enjoy here, and in bliss.
Besides, if holiness should first be found
In those whom God doth pardon, then the ground

Why we forgiven are would seem to be,
He first found holiness in thee and me;
But this the holy Scriptures will refute,
And prove that righteousness he doth impute
Without respect to goodness first in man;
For, to speak truth indeed, no goodness can
Be found in those that underneath the law
Do stand; for if God goodness in them saw,
Why doth he once and twice say, There is none
That righteous be; no, not so much as one;
None understandeth, none seek after God,
His ways they have not known, but have abode
In wickedness, unprofitably they
Must needs appear to be then every way.
Their throats an open sepulchre, also
Their mouths are full of filthy cursings too;
And bitterness, yea, underneath their lips
The asp hath poison. O how many slips
And falls in sin must such poor people have!
Now here's the holiness that should them save,
Or, as a preparation, go before,
To move God to do for them less or more?
No, grace must on thee righteousness bestow,
Or, else sin will for ever thee undo.
Sweet Paul this doctrine also doth express,
Where he saith, Some may have righteousness,
Though works they have not; and it thus may stand,
Grace by the promise gives what the command
Requireth us to do, and so are we
Quitted from doing, and by grace made free.

[OF HOLINESS OF LIFE.]

Now, then, if holiness thou wouldst obtain,
And wouldst a tender Christian man remain,
Keep faith in action, let that righteousness
That Christ fulfilled always have express
And clear distinction in thy heart, from all
That men by Scripture, or besides, it, call
Inherent gospel holiness, or what
Terms else they please to give it; for 'tis that,
And that alone, by which all graces come
Into the heart; for else there is no room
For ought but pride, presumption, or despair,
No love or other graces can be there.
Received you the Spirit, saith St. Paul,
By hearing, faith, or works? not works, and shall
No ways retain the same, except you do
Hear faith, embrace the same, and stick thereto.

[THE OPERATION OF FAITH.]

The word of faith unto me pardon brings,
Shows me the ground and reason whence it springs:
To wit, free grace, which moved God to give
His Son to die and bleed, that I might live
This word doth also loudly preach to me,
Though I a miserable sinner be,
Yet in this Son of God I stand complete,
Whose righteousness is without all deceit;
'Tis that which God himself delighteth in,
And that by which all his have saved been.

[OF LOVE TO GOD.]

When I do this begin to apprehend,
My heart, my soul, and mind, begins to bend
To God-ward, and sincerely for to love
His son, his ways, his people, and to move
With brokenness of spirit after him
Who broken was, and killed for my sin.
Now is mine heart grown holy, now it cleaves
To Jesus Christ my Lord, and now it leaves
Those ways that wicked be; it mourns because
It can conform no more unto the laws
Of God, who loved me when I was vile,
And of sweet Jesus, who did reconcile
Me unto justice by his precious blood,
When no way else was left to do me good.
If you would know how this can operate
Thus on the soul, I shall to you relate
A little farther what my soul hath seen
Since I have with the Lord acquainted been.
The word of grace, when it doth rightly seize
The spirit of a man, and so at ease
Doth set the soul, the Spirit of the Lord
Doth then with might accompany the word;
In which it sets forth Christ as crucified,
And by that means the Father pacified
With such a wretch was thou, and by this sight,
Thy guilt is in the first place put to flight,
For thus the Spirit doth expostulate:
Behold how God doth now communicate
(By changing of the person) grace to thee
A sinner, but to Christ great misery,
Though he the just one was, and so could not
Deserve this punishment; behold, then, what
The love of God is! how 'tis manifest,
And where the reason lies that thou art blest.
This doctrine being spoken to the heart,
Which also is made yield to every part
Thereof, it doth the same with sweetness fill,

And so doth sins and wickednesses kill;
For when the love of God is thus reveal'd,
And thy poor drooping spirit thereby seal'd,
And when thy heart, as dry ground, drinks this in
Unto the roots thereof, which nourish sin,
It smites them, as the worm did Jonah's gourd,
And makes them dwindle of their own accord,
And die away; instead of which there springs
Up life and love, and other holy things.
Besides, the Holy Spirit now is come,
And takes possession of thee as its home;
By which a war maintained always is
Against the old man and the deeds of his.

When God at first upon mount Sinai spake,
He made his very servant Moses quake;
But when he heard the law the second time,
His heart was comforted, his face did shine.
What was the reason of this difference,
Seeing no change was in the ordinance,
Although a change was in the manner, when
The second time he gave it unto men?
At first 'twas given in severity,
In thunder, blackness, darkness, tempest high,
In fiery flames it was delivered.
This struck both Moses and the host as dead;
But Moses, when he went into the mount
The second time, upon the same account
No fear, nor dread, nor shaking of his mind,
Do we in all the holy Scripture find;
But rather in his spirit he had rest,
And look'd upon himself as greatly blest.
He was put in the rock, he heard the name,
Which on the mount the Lord did thus proclaim:
The Lord, merciful, gracious, and more,
Long-suffering, and keeping up in store
Mercy for thousands, pardoning these things,
Iniquity, transgressions, and sins,
And holding guilty none but such as still
Refuse forgiveness, of rebellious will.

This proclamation better pleased him
Than all the thunder and the light'ning.
Which shook the mount, this rid him of his fear,
This made him bend, make haste, and worship there.

Jehoshaphat, when he was sore opprest
By Amnon and by Moab, and the rest
Of them that sought his life, no rest he found,
Until a word of faith became a ground
To stay himself upon; O, then they fell,

His very song became their passing-bell.
Then holiness of heart a consequence
Of faith in Christ is, for it flows from thence;
The love of Christ in truth constraineth us,
Of love sincerely to make judgment thus:
He for us died that for ever we
Might die to sin, and Christ his servants be.
O! nothing's like to the remembrance
Of what it is to have deliverance
From death and hell, which is of due our right,
Nothing, I say, like this to work delight
In holy things; this like live honey runs,
And needs no pressing out of honey-combs.

[LOVE INDUCING CHRISTIAN CONDUCT.]

Then understand my meaning by my words,
How sense of mercy unto faith affords
Both grace to sanctify, and holy make
That soul that of forgiveness doth partake.
Thus having briefly showed you what is
The way of life, or sanctity, of bliss,
I would not in conclusion have you think,
By what I say, that Christian men should drink
In these my words with lightness, or that they
Are now exempted from what every day
Their duty is. No, God doth still expect,
Yea, doth command, that they do not neglect
To pray, to read, to hear, and not dissent
From being sober, grave, and diligent
In watching, self-denial, and with fear
To serve him all the time thou livest here.
Indeed I have endeavoured to lay
Before your eyes the right and only way
Pardon to get, and also holiness,
Without which never think that God will bless
Thee with the kingdom he will give to those
That Christ embrace, and holy lives do choose
To live, while here all others go astray,
And shall in time to come be cast away.

FROM MOUNT EBAL.

Thus having heard from Gerizzim, I shall
Next come to Ebal, and you thither call,
Not there to curse you, but to let you hear
How God doth curse that soul that shall appear
An unbelieving man, a graceless wretch;
Because he doth continue in the breach
Of Moses' law, and also doth neglect

To close with Jesus; him will God reject
And cast behind him; for of right his due
Is that from whence all miseries ensue.
Cursed, saith he, are thy that do transgress
The least of my commandments, more or less.
Nothing that written is must broken be,
But always must be kept unto by thee,
And must fulfilled be; for here no man
Can look God in the face, or ever stand
Before the judgment-seat; for if they be
Convict, condemned too assuredly.
Now keep this law no mortal creature can,
For they already do, as guilty, stand
Before the God that gave it; so that they
Obnoxious to the curse lie every day,
Which also they must feel for certainty,
If unto Jesus Christ they do not fly.
Hence, then, as they for ever shall be blest,
That do by faith upon the promise rest,
So peace unto the wicked there is none;
'Tis wrath and death that they must feed upon.

That what I say may some impression make
On carnal hearts, that they in time may take
That course that best will prove when time is done,
These lines I add to what I have begun.

First, thou must know that God, as he is love
So he is justice, therefore cannot move,
Or in the least be brought to favour those
His holiness and justice doth oppose.

For though thou mayst imagine in thy heart
That God is this or that, yet if thou art
At all besides the truth of what he is,
And so dost build thy hope for life amiss,
Still he the same abideth, and will be
The same, the same for ever unto thee.

As God is true unto his promise, so
Unto his threat'ning he is faithful too.
Cease to be God he must, if he should break
One tittle that his blessed mouth did speak.

Now, then, none can be saved but the men
With whom the Godhead is contented when
It them beholds with the severest eye
Of justice, holiness, and yet can spy
No fault nor blemish in them; these be they
That must be saved, as the Scriptures say.

If this be true, as 'tis assuredly,
Woe be to them that wicked live and die;
Those that as far from holiness have been
All their life long as if no eye had seen
Their doings here, or as if God did not
At all regard, or in the least mind what,
Wherein, or how they did his law transgress,
Either by this or other wickedness;
But how deceived these poor creatures are,
They then shall know when they their burthen bear.

Alas, our God is a consuming fire·
So is his law, by which he doth require
That thou submit to him, and if thou be
Not in that justice found that can save thee
From all and every sentence which he spake
Upon mount Sinai, then as one that brake
It, thou the flames thereof shall quickly find
As scourges thee to lash, while sins do bind
Thee hand and foot, for ever to endure
The strokes of vengeance for thy life impure.

What I have said will yet evinced be,
And manifest abundantly to thee,
If what I have already spoken to
Be joined with these lines that do ensue.
Justice discovers its antipathy
Against profaneness and malignity.
Not only by the law it gave to men,
And threatenings thereunto annexed then.
But inasmuch as long before that day,
He did prepare for such as go astray,
That dreadful, that so much amazing place–
Hell, with its torments–for those men that grace
And holiness of life slight and disdain,
There to bemoan themselves with hellish pain.

This place, also, the pains so dismal be,
Both as to name and nature, that in me
It is not to express the damning wights,
The hellish torture, and the fearful plights
Thereof; for as intolerable they
Must needs be found, by those that disobey
The Lord, so can no word or thought express
Unto the full the height of that distress;
Such miserable caitiffs, that shall there
Rebukes of vengeance, for transgressions bear.

Indeed the holy Scriptures do make use
Of many metaphors, that do conduce
Much to the symbolizing of the place,

Unto our apprehension; but the case–
The sad, the woful case–of those that lie
As racked there in endless misery,
By all similitudes no mortals may
Set forth in its own nature; for I say
Similitudes are but a shade, and show
Of those or that they signify to you.
The fire that doth within thine oven burn,
The prison where poor people sit and mourn,
Chains, racks, and darkness, and such others, be
As painting on the wall, to let thee see
By word and figures the extremity
Of such as shall within these burnings lie.

But certainly, if wickedness and sin
Had only foolish toys and trifles been,
And if God had not greatly hated it,
Yea, could he any ways thereof admit,
And let it pass, he would not thus have done.
He doth not use to punish any one
With any place or punishment that is
Above or sharper than the sin of his
Hath merited, and justice seeth due;
Read sin, then, by the death that doth ensue.

Most men do judge of sin, not by the fruits
It bears and bringeth forth, but as it suits
Their carnal and deluded hearts, that be
With sensual pleasures eaten up; but he
That now so judgeth, shortly shall perceive
That God will judge thereof himself, and leave
Such men no longer to their carnal lusts,
To judge of wickedness, and of the just
And righteous punishment that doth of right
Belong thereto; and will, too, in despite
Of all their carnal reason, justify
Himself, in their eternal misery.
Then hell will be no fancy, neither will
Men's sins be pleasant to them; but so ill
And bitter, yea, so bitter, that none can
Fully express the same, or ever stand
Under the burden it will on them lay,
When they from life and bliss are sent away.

When I have thought how often God doth speak
Of their destruction, who HIS law do break;
And when the nature of the punishment
I find so dreadful, and that God's intent,
Yea, resolution is, it to inflict
On every sinner that shall stand convict,
I have amazed been, yet to behold,

To see poor sinners yet with sin so bold,
That like the horse that to the battle runs,
Without all fear, and that no danger shuns,
Till down he falls. O resolute attempts!
O sad, amazing, damnable events!
The end of such proceedings needs must be,
From which, O Lord, save and deliver me.
But if thou think that God thy noble race
Will more respect, than into such a place
To put thee; hold, though thou his offspring be,
And so art lovely, yet sin hath made thee
Another kind of creature than when thou
Didst from his fingers drop, and therefore now
Thy first creation stands thee in no stead;
Thou hast transgressed, and in very deed
Set God against thee, who is infinite,
And that for certain never will forget
Thy sins, nor favour thee if thou shalt die
A graceless man; this is thy misery.

When angels sinned, though of higher race
Than thou, and also put in higher place,
Yet them he spared not, but cast them down
From heaven to hell; where also they lie bound
In everlasting chains, and no release
Shall ever have, but wrath, that shall increase
Upon them, to their everlasting woe.
As for the state they were exalted to,
That will by no means mitigate their fear,
But aggravate their hellish torment here;
For he that highest stands, if he shall fall,
His danger needs must be the great'st of all.
Now if God noble angels did not spare
Because they did transgress, will he forbear
Poor dust and ashes? Will he suffer them
To break his law, and sin, and not condemn
Them for so doing? Let not man deceive
Himself or others; they that do bereave
Themselves by sin of happiness, shall be
Cut off by justice, and have misery.

Witness his great severity upon
The world that first was planted, wherein none
But only eight the deluge did escape,
All others of that vengeance did partake;
The reason was, that world ungodly stood
Before him, therefore he did send the flood,
Which swept them all away. A just reward
For their most wicked ways against the Lord,
Who could no longer bear them and their ways,
Therefore into their bosom vengeance pays.

We read of Sodom, and Gomorrah too,
What judgments they for sin did undergo;
How God from heaven did fire upon them rain,
Because they would not wicked ways refrain;
Condemning of them with an overthrow,
And turned them to ashes. Who can know
The miseries that these poor people felt
While they did underneath those burnings melt?
Now these, and many more that I could name,
That have been made partakers of the flame
And sword of justice, God did then cut off,
And make examples unto all that scoff
At holiness, or do the gospel slight;
And long it will not be before the night
And judgment, painted out by what he did
To Sodom and Gomorrah, fulfilled
Upon such sinners be, that they may now
That God doth hate the sin, and persons too.
Of such as still rebellious shall abide,
Although they now at judgment may deride.

FOOTNOTES:

[1] On the reverse of the title-page is the following singular advertisement:–'This author having published many books, which have gone off very well, there are certain ballad-sellers about Newgate, and on London Bridge, who have put the two first letters of this author's name, and his effigies, to their rhymes and ridiculous books, suggesting to the world as if they were his. Now know, that this author publisheth his name at large to all his books; and what you shall see otherwise, he disowns.'–Ed.

[2] 'Convert,' for 'be ye converted,' was a common mode of speech in Bunyan's time. It is so used in Holy Writ, Isaiah 6:10.–Ed.

[3] Armorial bearings as now worn by heralds embroidered on the tabard or coat.–Ed.

[4] A common custom when death takes place. The two great toes are tied together, to make the body look decent; and formerly the hands were placed with the palms together, as if in the attitude of prayer, and were kept in that posture by tying the thumbs together.–Ed.

[5] Without fail, or in spite of all hindrance.–Ed.

[6] Alluding to wrestlers. Some modes of throwing each other down are called fair, others foul or unfair.–Ed.

[7] Sincerity is the fountain and source of all real inquiries after truth, holiness, and heaven. It leads to personal examination of God's Word, which leads us from the complexity of human inventions to the simplicity of the gospel.–Ed

[8] The exact spelling of Bunyan is here followed; but whether he meant 'coped,' 'covered,' or 'cooped'–inclosed, or shut in–must be left to the reader's judgment. I prefer the latter.–Ed.

[9] Fit, convenient. 'Deft' is now obsolete.–Ed.

[10] Full of fear and dread. Bunyan, in his Holy War, brings his immense armies of doubters, under General Incredulity, from Hell-gate Hill.–Ed.

[11] Quick, nimble, active, powerful spirits. Wight is now obsolete, except in irony; see Imperial Dictionary.–Ed.

[12] See note on verse fifty of the Meditations on Heaven.–Ed.

[13] This is a common temptation. Job felt it, and murmured at having been born, Job 3:3, and 10:18, 19. Jeremiah passed through the same experience, Jeremiah 20:14, 15. Bunyan had the same bitter feelings, and wished himself a dog or toad; see Grace Abounding, No. 104. Colonel Gardener was similarly tried. How awful is the havoc that sin has made with human happiness.–Ed.

[14] The finest particles or atoms of matter–

'As thick, as numberless 'As the gay motes that people the sunbeams.'–Milton.–Ed.

[15] How does this remind us of the awfully impressive cries of the man in the iron cage–'O, eternity, eternity! how shall I grapple with the misery that I must meet with in eternity!' 'A thousand deaths live in him, he not dead.'–Ed.

[16] From the Saxon scendan, to violate, spoil, revile; see Imperial Dictionary.–Ed.

[17] Altered by poetical license from 'bran.' Chaucer, in one instance, spells it 'bren,' to rhyme with men.–Ed.

[18] This evidently refers to a coin value four-penny half-penny, and, like a cracked groat, not so much prized as good coin. In Turner's Remarkable Providences, folio, 1697, pages 28, is a very singular allusion to one of these coins:–'Christian, the wife of R. Green, of Brenham, Somersetshire, in 1663, made a covenant with the devil. He pricked the fourth finger off her right hand, between the middle and upper joint, and took two drops of her blood on his finger, giving her four-pence half-penny. He then vanished, leaving a smell of brimstone behind.'–Ed.

Advertisement by the Editor

Some degree of mystery hangs over these Divine Emblems for children, and many years' diligent researches have not enabled me completely to solve it. That they were written by Bunyan, there cannot be the slightest doubt.

'Manner and matter, too, are all his own.'[1]

But no book, under the title of Divine Emblems, is mentioned in any catalogue or advertisements of Bunyan's works, published during his life; nor in those more complete lists printed by his personal friends, immediately after his death. In all these lists, as well as in many advertisement, both before, and shortly after Mr. Bunyan's death, a little book for children is constantly introduced, which, judging from the title, must have been similar to, if not the same as, these Emblems; but the Editor has not been able to discover a copy of the first edition, although every inquiry has been made for it, both in the United Kingdom and America. It was advertised in 1688, as Country Rhymes for Children, upon seventy-four things.[2] It is also advertised, in the same year, as A Book for Boys and Girls, or Country Rhymes for Children, price 6d.[3] In 1692, it is included in Charles Doe's catalogue table of all Mr. Bunyan's books, appended to The Struggler for their preservation, No. 36; Meditations on seventy-four things, published in 1685, and not reprinted during the author's life. In Charles Doe's second catalogue of all Mr. Bunyan's books, appended to the first edition of the Heavenly Footman, March 1698, it is No. 37. A Book for Boys and Girls, or Country Rhymes for Children, in verse, on seventy-four things. This catalogue describes every work, word for word, as it is in the several title pages. In 1707 it had reached a third edition, and was 'ornamented with cuts';[4] and the title is altered to A Book for Boys and Girls, or Temporal Things Spiritualized, with cuts. In 1720, it was advertised, 'price, bound, 6d.'[5] In Keach's Glorious Lover, it is advertised by Marshall, in 12mo. price 1s. In 1724, it assumed its present title, and from that time was repeatedly advertised as Divine Emblems, or Temporal Things Spiritualized, fitted for the use of boys and girls, adorned with cuts.

By indefatigable exertions, my excellent friend and brother collector of old English bibles, James Dix, Esq., Bristol, has just discovered and presented to me the second edition of this very rare little volume, in fine preservation, from which it appears, that in 1701, the title page was altered from Country Rhymes and Meditations, to A Book for Boys and Girls, or Temporal Things Spiritualized. It has no cuts, but, with that exception, it contains exactly the same subjects as the subsequent editions published under the more popular title of Divine Emblems.

The only difficulty that remains is to discover seventy-four meditations in the forty-nine Emblems. This may be readily done, if the subjects of meditation are drawn out. Thus, the first emblem contains meditations on two things, the Barren Fig-tree, and God's Vineyard. So the second has a meditation on the Lark and the Fowler, and another on the comparison between the Fowler and Satan. Upon this plan, the volume contains exactly seventy-four meditations.

Under the title of Divine Emblems, it has passed through a multitude of editions, and many thousand copies have been circulated. It was patronized in those early efforts of the Religious Tract Society, which have been so abundantly blessed in introducing wholesome food to the young, instead of the absurd romances which formerly poisoned the infant and youthful mind.

Among these numerous editions, two deserve special notice. The first of these was published in 1757, 'on a curious paper, and good letter, with new cuts.' It has a singular preface, signed J. D., addressed 'to the great Boys, in folio, and the little ones in coats.' The first eight pages are occupied with a dissertation on the origin of language, perhaps arising from a line in the dialogue between a sinner and spider, 'My name entailed is to my creation.' In this preface, he learnedly attempts to prove that language was the gift of God by revelation, and not a gradual acquirement of man as his wants multiplied. The other remarkable edition was published about 1790.[6] It is, both the text and cuts, printed from copperplate engravings, very handsomely executed. This is an honour conferred upon very few authors;[7] nor was it ever conferred upon one more worthy the highest veneration of man than is the immortal allegorist.

The number of editions which have been printed of these little engaging poems, is a proof of the high estimation in which they have been held for nearly one hundred and seventy years; and the great rarity of the early copies shows the eager interest with which they have been read by children until utterly destroyed.

The cuts were at first exceedingly coarse and rude, but were much improved in the more modern copies. Those to Mason's edition are handsome. The engraver has dressed all his actors in the costume of the time of George the Third; the women with hooped petticoats and high head dresses; clergymen with five or six tier wigs; men with cocked hats and queues; and female servants with mob caps. That to Emblem Fifteen, upon the sacraments, is peculiarly droll; the artist, forgetting that the author was a Baptist, represents a baby brought to the font to be christened! and two persons kneeling before the body of our Lord!

GEO. OFFOR.

COURTEOUS READER,

The title page will show, if there thou look,
Who are the proper subjects of this book.
They're boys and girls of all sorts and degrees,
From those of age to children on the knees.
Thus comprehensive am I in my notions,
They tempt me to it by their childish motions.
We now have boys with beards, and girls that be
Big[8]as old women, wanting gravity.

Then do not blame me, 'cause I thus describe them.
Flatter I may not, lest thereby I bribe them
To have a better judgment of themselves,
Than wise men have of babies on their shelves.[9]
Their antic tricks, fantastic modes, and way,
Show they, like very boys and girls, do play
With all the frantic fopperies of this age,
And that in open view, as on a stage;
Our bearded men do act like beardless boys;
Our women please themselves with childish toys.

Our ministers, long time, by word and pen,
Dealt with them, counting them not boys, but men.
Thunderbolts they shot at them and their toys,
But hit them not, 'cause they were girls and boys.
The better charg'd, the wider still they shot,
Or else so high, these dwarfs they touched not.
Instead of men, they found them girls and boys,
Addict to nothing as to childish toys.

Wherefore, good reader, that I save them may,
I now with them the very dotterel[10] play;
And since at gravity they make a tush,

My very beard I cast behind a bush;
And like a fool stand fing'ring of their toys,
And all to show them they are girls and boys.

Nor do I blush, although I think some may
Call me a baby, 'cause I with them play.
I do't to show them how each fingle-fangle
On which they doting are, their souls entangle,
As with a web, a trap, a gin, or snare;
And will destroy them, have they not a care.

Paul seemed to play the fool, that he might gain
Those that were fools indeed, if not in grain;[11]
And did it by their things, that they might know
Their emptiness, and might be brought unto
What would them save from sin and vanity,
A noble act, and full of honesty.
Yet he nor I would like them be in vice,
While by their playthings I would them entice,
To mount their thoughts from what are childish toys,
To heaven, for that's prepared for girls and boys.
Nor do I so confine myself to these,
As to shun graver things; I seek to please
Those more compos'd with better things than toys;
Though thus I would be catching girls and boys.

Wherefore, if men have now a mind to look,
Perhaps their graver fancies may be took
With what is here, though but in homely rhymes:
But he who pleases all must rise betimes.
Some, I persuade me, will be finding fault,
Concluding, here I trip, and there I halt:
No doubt some could those grovelling notions raise
By fine-spun terms, that challenge might the bays.
But should all men be forc'd to lay aside
Their brains that cannot regulate the tide
By this or that man's fancy, we should have
The wise unto the fool become a slave.
What though my text seems mean, my morals be
Grave, as if fetch'd from a sublimer tree.
And if some better handle[12] can a fly,
Than some a text, why should we then deny
Their making proof, or good experiment,
Of smallest things, great mischiefs to prevent?

Wise Solomon did fools to piss-ants[13] send,
To learn true wisdom, and their lies to mend.
Yea, God by swallows, cuckoos, and the ass,[14]
Shows they are fools who let that season pass,
Which he put in their hand, that to obtain
Which is both present and eternal gain.

I think the wiser sort my rhymes may slight,
But what care I, the foolish will delight
To read them, and the foolish God has chose,
And doth by foolish things their minds compose,
And settle upon that which is divine;
Great things, by little ones, are made to shine.

I could, were I so pleas'd, use higher strains:
And for applause on tenters[15] stretch my brains.
But what needs that? the arrow, out of sight,
Does not the sleeper, nor the watchman fright;
To shoot too high doth but make children gaze,
'Tis that which hits the man doth him amaze.

And for the inconsiderableness
Of things, by which I do my mind express,
May I by them bring some good thing to pass,
As Samson, with the jawbone of an ass;
Or as brave Shamgar, with his ox's goad
(Both being things not manly, nor for war in mode),
I have my end, though I myself expose
To scorn; God will have glory in the close.

J.B.

A BOOK FOR BOYS AND GIRLS, &c.

DIVINE EMBLEMS, OR TEMPORAL THINGS SPIRITUALIZED, &c.

I

UPON THE BARREN FIG-TREE IN GOD'S VINEYARD

What, barren here! in this so good a soil?
The sight of this doth make God's heart recoil
From giving thee his blessing; barren tree,
Bear fruit, or else thine end will cursed be!
Art thou not planted by the water-side?
Know'st not thy Lord by fruit is glorified?
The sentence is, Cut down the barren tree:
Bear fruit, or else thine end will cursed be.
Hast thou been digg'd about and dunged too,
Will neither patience nor yet dressing do?
The executioner is come, O tree,
Bear fruit, or else thine end will cursed be!
He that about thy roots takes pains to dig,
Would, if on thee were found but one good fig,
Preserve thee from the axe: but, barren tree,
Bear fruit, or else thy end will cursed be!

The utmost end of patience is at hand,
'Tis much if thou much longer here doth stand.
O cumber-ground, thou art a barren tree.
Bear fruit, or else thine end will cursed be!
Thy standing nor they name will help at all;
When fruitful trees are spared, thou must fall.
The axe is laid unto thy roots, O tree!
Bear fruit, or else thine end will cursed be.

II

UPON THE LARK AND THE FOWLER

Thou simple bird, what makes thou here to play?
Look, there's the fowler, pr'ythee come away.
Do'st not behold the net? Look there, 'tis spread,
Venture a little further, thou art dead.
Is there not room enough in all the field
For thee to play in, but thou needs must yield
To the deceitful glitt'ring of a glass,
Plac'd betwixt nets, to bring thy death to pass?
Bird, if thou art so much for dazzling light,
Look, there's the sun above thee; dart upright;
Thy nature is to soar up to the sky,
Why wilt thou come down to the nets and die?
Take no heed to the fowler's tempting call;
This whistle, he enchanteth birds withal.
Or if thou see'st a live bird in his net,
Believe she's there, 'cause hence she cannot get.
Look how he tempteth thee with is decoy,
That he may rob thee of thy life, thy joy.
Come, pr'ythee bird, I pr'ythee come away,
Why should this net thee take, when 'scape thou may?
Hadst thou not wings, or were thy feathers pull'd,
Or wast thou blind, or fast asleep wer't lull'd,
The case would somewhat alter, but for thee,
Thy eyes are ope, and thou hast wings to flee.
Remember that thy song is in thy rise,
Not in thy fall; earth's not thy paradise.
Keep up aloft, then, let thy circuits be
Above, where birds from fowler's nets are free.

Comparison.

This fowler is an emblem of the devil,
His nets and whistle, figures of all evil.
His glass an emblem is of sinful pleasure,
And his decoy of who counts sin a treasure.
This simple lark's a shadow of a saint,
Under allurings, ready now to faint.

This admonisher a true teacher is,
Whose works to show the soul the snare and bliss,
And how it may this fowler's net escape,
And not commit upon itself this rape.

III

UPON THE VINE-TREE

What is the vine, more than another tree?
Nay most, than it, more tall, more comely be
What workman thence will take a beam or pin,
To make ought which may be delighted in?
Its excellency in its fruit doth lie:
A fruitless vine, it is not worth a fly.

Comparison.

What are professors more than other men?
Nothing at all. Nay, there's not one in ten,
Either for wealth, or wit, that may compare,
In many things, with some that carnal are.
Good are they, if they mortify their sin,
But without that, they are not worth a pin.

IV

MEDITATIONS UPON AN EGG

I
The egg's no chick by falling from the hen;
Nor man a Christian, till he's born again.
The egg's at first contained in the shell;
Men, afore grace, in sins and darkness dwell.
The egg, when laid, by warmth is made a chicken,
And Christ, by grace, those dead in sin doth quicken.
The egg, when first a chick, the shell's its prison;
So's flesh to the soul, who yet with Christ is risen.
The shell doth crack, the chick doth chirp and peep,
The flesh decays, as men do pray and weep.
The shell doth break, the chick's at liberty,
The flesh falls off, the soul mounts up on high
But both do not enjoy the self-same plight;
The soul is safe, the chick now fears the kite.

II
But chicks from rotten eggs do not proceed,
Nor is a hypocrite a saint indeed.
The rotten egg, though underneath the hen,

If crack'd, stinks, and is loathsome unto men.
Nor doth her warmth make what is rotten sound;
What's rotten, rotten will at last be found.
The hypocrite, sin has him in possession,
He is a rotten egg under profession.

III

Some eggs bring cockatrices; and some men
Seem hatch'd and brooded in the viper's den.
Some eggs bring wild-fowls; and some men there be
As wild as are the wildest fowls that flee.
Some eggs bring spiders, and some men appear
More venom'd than the worst of spiders are.[16]
Some eggs bring piss-ants, and some seem to me
As much for trifles as the piss-ants be.
Thus divers eggs do produce divers shapes,
As like some men as monkeys are like apes.
But this is but an egg, were it a chick,
Here had been legs, and wings, and bones to pick.

V

OF FOWLS FLYING IN THE AIR

Methinks I see a sight most excellent,
All sorts of birds fly in the firmament:
Some great, some small, all of a divers kind,
Mine eye affecting, pleasant to my mind.
Look how they tumble in the wholesome air,
Above the world of worldlings, and their care.
And as they divers are in bulk and hue,
So are they in their way of flying too.
So many birds, so many various things
Tumbling i' the element upon their wings.

Comparison.

These birds are emblems of those men that shall
Ere long possess the heavens, their all in all.
They are each of a diverse shape and kind,
To teach we of all nations there shall find.
They are some great, some little, as we see,
To show some great, some small, in glory be.[17]
Their flying diversely, as we behold,
Do show saints' joys will there be manifold;
Some glide, some mount, some flutter, and some do,
In a mix'd way of flying, glory too.
And all to show each saint, to his content,
Shall roll and tumble in that firmament.

VI

UPON THE LORD'S PRAYER

Our Father which in heaven art,
Thy name be always hallowed;
Thy kingdom come, thy will be done;
Thy heavenly path be followed
By us on earth as 'tis with thee,
We humbly pray;
And let our bread us given be,
From day to day.
Forgive our debts as we forgive
Those that to us indebted are:
Into temptation lead us not,[18]
But save us from the wicked snare.
The kingdom's thine, the power too,
We thee adore;
The glory also shall be thine
For evermore.

VII

MEDITATIONS UPON PEEP OF DAY

I oft, though it be peep of day, don't know
Whether 'tis night, whether 'tis day or no.
I fancy that I see a little light,
But cannot yet distinguish day from night;
I hope, I doubt, but steady yet I be not,
I am not at a point, the sun I see not.
Thus 'tis with such who grace but now[19] possest,
They know not yet if they be cursed or blest.

VIII

UPON THE FLINT IN THE WATER

This flint, time out of mind, has there abode,
Where crystal streams make their continual road.
Yet it abides a flint as much as 'twere
Before it touched the water, or came there
Its hard obdurateness is not abated,
'Tis not at all by water penetrated.
Though water hath a soft'ning virtue in't,
This stone it can't dissolve, for 'tis a flint.
Yea, though it in the water doth remain,
It doth its fiery nature still retain.

If you oppose it with its opposite,
At you, yea, in your face, its fire 'twill spit.

Comparison.

This flint an emblem is of those that lie,
Like stones, under the Word, until they die.
Its crystal streams have not their nature changed,
They are not, from their lusts, by grace estranged.

IX

UPON THE FISH IN THE WATER

I
The water is the fish's element;
Take her from thence, none can her death prevent;
And some have said, who have transgressors been,
As good not be, as to be kept from sin.

II
The water is the fish's element:
Leave her but there, and she is well content.
So's he, who in the path of life doth plod,
Take all, says he, let me but have my God.

III
The water is the fish's element,
Her sportings there to her are excellent;
So is God's service unto holy men,
They are not in their element till then.

X

UPON THE SWALLOW

This pretty bird, O! how she flies and sings,[20]
But could she do so if she had not wings?
Her wings bespeak my faith, her songs my peace;
When I believe and sing my doubtings cease.

XI

UPON THE BEE

The bee goes out, and honey home doth bring,
And some who seek that honey find a sting.
Now would'st thou have the honey, and be free

From stinging, in the first place kill the bee.

Comparison.

This bee an emblem truly is of sin,
Whose sweet, unto a many, death hath been.
Now would'st have sweet from sin and yet not die,
Do thou it, in the first place, mortify.

UPON A LOWERING MORNING

Well, with the day I see the clouds appear,
And mix the light with darkness everywhere;
This threatening is, to travellers that go
Long journeys, slabby rain they'll have, or snow.
Else, while I gaze, the sun doth with his beams
Belace the clouds, as 'twere with bloody streams;
This done, they suddenly do watery grow,
And weep, and pour their tears out where they go.

Comparison.

Thus 'tis when gospel light doth usher in
To us both sense of grace and sense of sin;
Yea, when it makes sin red with Christ's blood,
Then we can weep till weeping does us good.

XIII

UPON OVER-MUCH NICENESS

'Tis much to see how over nice some are
About the body and household affair,
While what's of worth they slightly pass it by,
Not doing, or doing it slovenly.
Their house must be well furnished, be in print,[21]
Meanwhile their soul lies ley,[22] has no good in't.
Its outside also they must beautify,
When in it there's scarce common honesty.
Their bodies they must have tricked up and trim,
Their inside full of filth up to the brim.
Upon their clothes there must not be a spot,
But is their lives more than one common blot.
How nice, how coy are some about their diet,
That can their crying souls with hogs'-meat quiet.
All drest must to a hair be, else 'tis naught,
While of the living bread they have no thought.

Thus for their outside they are clean and nice,
While their poor inside stinks with sin and vice.

XIV

MEDITATIONS UPON A CANDLE

Man's like a candle in a candlestick,
Made up of tallow and a little wick;
And as the candle when it is not lighted,
So is he who is in his sins benighted.
Nor can a man his soul with grace inspire,
More than can candles set themselves on fire.
Candles receive their light from what they are not;
Men grace from Him for whom at first they care not.
We manage candles when they take the fire;
God men, when he with grace doth them inspire.
And biggest candles give the better light,
As grace on biggest sinners shines most bright.
The candle shines to make another see,
A saint unto his neighbour light should be.
The blinking candle we do much despise,
Saints dim of light are high in no man's eyes.
Again, though it may seem to some a riddle,
We use to light our candles at the middle.[23]
True light doth at the candle's end appear,
And grace the heart first reaches by the ear.
But 'tis the wick the fire doth kindle on,
As 'tis the heart that grace first works upon.
Thus both do fasten upon what's the main,
And so their life and vigour do maintain.
The tallow makes the wick yield to the fire,
And sinful flesh doth make the soul desire
That grace may kindle on it, in it burn;
So evil makes the soul from evil turn.[24]
But candles in the wind are apt to flare,
And Christians, in a tempest, to despair.
The flame also with smoke attended is,
And in our holy lives there's much amiss.
Sometimes a thief will candle-light annoy,
And lusts do seek our graces to destroy.
What brackish is will make a candle sputter;
'Twixt sin and grace there's oft' a heavy clutter.
Sometimes the light burns dim, 'cause of the snuff,
Sometimes it is blown quite out with a puff;
But watchfulness preventeth both these evils,
Keeps candles light, and grace in spite of devils.
Nor let not snuffs nor puffs make us to doubt,
Our candles may be lighted, though puffed out.
The candle in the night doth all excel,

Nor sun, nor moon, nor stars, then shine so well.
So is the Christian in our hemisphere,
Whose light shows others how their course to steer.
When candles are put out, all's in confusion;
Where Christians are not, devils make intrusion.
Then happy are they who such candles have,
All others dwell in darkness and the grave.
But candles that do blink within the socket,
And saints, whose eyes are always in their pocket,
Are much alike; such candles make us fumble,
And at such saints good men and bad do stumble.[25]
Good candles don't offend, except sore eyes,
Nor hurt, unless it be the silly flies.
Thus none like burning candles in the night,
Nor ought[26] to holy living for delight.
But let us draw towards the candle's end:
The fire, you see, doth wick and tallow spend,
As grace man's life until his glass is run,
And so the candle and the man is done.
The man now lays him down upon his bed,
The wick yields up its fire, and so is dead.
The candle now extinct is, but the man
By grace mounts up to glory, there to stand.

XV

UPON THE SACRAMENTS

Two sacraments I do believe there be,
Baptism and the Supper of the Lord;
Both mysteries divine, which do to me,
By God's appointment, benefit afford.
But shall they be my God, or shall I have
Of them so foul and impious a thought,
To think that from the curse they can me save?
Bread, wine, nor water, me no ransom bought.[27]

XVI

UPON THE SUN'S REFLECTION UPON THE CLOUDS IN A FAIR MORNING

Look yonder, ah! methinks mine eyes do see
Clouds edged with silver, as fine garments be;
They look as if they saw that golden face
That makes black clouds most beautiful with grace.
Unto the saints' sweet incense, or their prayer,
These smoky curdled clouds I do compare.
For as these clouds seem edged, or laced with gold,
Their prayers return with blessings manifold.

UPON APPAREL

God gave us clothes to hide our nakedness,
And we by them do it expose to view.
Our pride and unclean minds to an excess,
By our apparel, we to others show.[28]

THE SINNER AND THE SPIDER

Sinner.
What black, what ugly crawling thing art thou?

Spider.
I am a spider–

Sinner.
A spider, ay, also a filthy creature.

Spider.
Not filthy as thyself in name or feature.
My name entailed is to my creation,
My features from the God of thy salvation.

Sinner.
I am a man, and in God's image made,
I have a soul shall neither die nor fade,
God has possessed me[29] with human reason,
Speak not against me lest thou speakest treason.
For if I am the image of my Maker,
Of slanders laid on me He is partaker.

Spider.
I know thou art a creature far above me,
Therefore I shun, I fear, and also love thee.
But though thy God hath made thee such a creature,
Thou hast against him often played the traitor.
Thy sin has fetched thee down: leave off to boast;
Nature thou hast defiled, God's image lost.
Yea, thou thyself a very beast hast made,
And art become like grass, which soon doth fade.
Thy soul, thy reason, yea, thy spotless state,
Sin has subjected to th' most dreadful fate.
But I retain my primitive condition,
I've all but what I lost by thy ambition.

Sinner.
Thou venomed thing, I know not what to call thee,
The dregs of nature surely did befall thee,
Thou wast made of the dross and scum of all,
Man hates thee; doth, in scorn, thee spider call.

Spider.
My venom's good for something, 'cause God made it,
Thy sin hath spoiled thy nature, doth degrade it.
Of human virtues, therefore, though I fear thee,
I will not, though I might, despise and jeer thee.
Thou say'st I am the very dregs of nature,
Thy sin's the spawn of devils, 'tis no creature.
Thou say'st man hates me 'cause I am a spider,
Poor man, thou at thy God art a derider;
My venom tendeth to my preservation,
Thy pleasing follies work out thy damnation.
Poor man, I keep the rules of my creation,
Thy sin has cast thee headlong from thy station.
I hurt nobody willingly, but thou
Art a self-murderer; thou know'st not how
To do what good is; no, thou lovest evil;
Thou fliest God's law, adherest to the devil.[30]

Sinner.
Ill-shaped creature, there's antipathy
'Twixt man and spiders, 'tis in vain to lie;
I hate thee, stand off, if thou dost come nigh me,
I'll crush thee with my foot; I do defy thee.

Spider.
They are ill-shaped, who warped are by sin,
Antipathy in thee hath long time been
To God; no marvel, then, if me, his creature,
Thou dost defy, pretending name and feature.
But why stand off? My presence shall not throng thee,
'Tis not my venom, but thy sin doth wrong thee.
Come, I will teach thee wisdom, do but hear me,
I was made for thy profit, do not fear me.
But if thy God thou wilt not hearken to,
What can the swallow, ant, or spider do?
Yet I will speak, I can but be rejected,
Sometimes great things by small means are effected.
Hark, then, though man is noble by creation,
He's lapsed now to such degeneration,
Is so besotted and so careless grown,
As not to grieve though he has overthrown
Himself, and brought to bondage everything
Created, from the spider to the king.
This we poor sensitives do feel and see;

For subject to the curse you made us be.
Tread not upon me, neither from me go;
'Tis man which has brought all the world to woe,
The law of my creation bids me teach thee;
I will not for thy pride to God impeach thee.
I spin, I weave, and all to let thee see,
Thy best performances but cobwebs be.
Thy glory now is brought to such an ebb,
It doth not much excel the spider's web;
My webs becoming snares and traps for flies,
Do set the wiles of hell before thine eyes;
Their tangling nature is to let thee see,
Thy sins too of a tangling nature be.
My den, or hole, for that 'tis bottomless,
Doth of damnation show the lastingness.
My lying quiet until the fly is catch'd,
Shows secretly hell hath thy ruin hatch'd.
In that I on her seize, when she is taken,
I show who gathers whom God hath forsaken.
The fly lies buzzing in my web to tell
Thee how the sinners roar and howl in hell.
Now, since I show thee all these mysteries,
How canst thou hate me, or me scandalize?

Sinner.
Well, well; I no more will be a derider,
I did not look for such things from a spider.

Spider.
Come, hold thy peace; what I have yet to say,
If heeded, help thee may another day.
Since I an ugly ven'mous creature be,
There is some semblance 'twixt vile man and me.
My wild and heedless runnings are like those
Whose ways to ruin do their souls expose.
Daylight is not my time, I work in th' night,
To show they are like me who hate the light.
The maid sweeps one web down, I make another,
To show how heedless ones convictions smother;
My web is no defence at all to me,
Nor will false hopes at judgment be to thee.

Sinner.
O spider, I have heard thee, and do wonder
A spider should thus lighten and thus thunder.

Spider.
Do but hold still, and I will let thee see
Yet in my ways more mysteries there be.
Shall not I do thee good, if I thee tell,
I show to thee a four-fold way to hell;

For, since I set my web in sundry places,
I show men go to hell in divers traces.
One I set in the window, that I might
Show some go down to hell with gospel light.
One I set in a corner, as you see,
To show how some in secret snared be.
Gross webs great store I set in darksome places,
To show how many sin with brazen faces;
Another web I set aloft on high,
To show there's some professing men must die.
Thus in my ways God wisdom doth conceal,
And by my ways that wisdom doth reveal.
I hide myself when I for flies do wait,
So doth the devil when he lays his bait;
If I do fear the losing of my prey,
I stir me, and more snares upon her lay:
This way and that her wings and legs I tie,
That, sure as she is catch'd, so she must die.
But if I see she's like to get away,
Then with my venom I her journey stay.
All which my ways the devil imitates
To catch men, 'cause he their salvation hates.

Sinner.
O spider, thou delight'st me with thy skill!
I pr'ythee spit this venom at me still.

Spider.
I am a spider, yet I can possess
The palace of a king, where happiness
So much abounds. Nor when I do go thither,
Do they ask what, or whence I come, or whither
I make my hasty travels; no, not they;
They let me pass, and I go on my way.
I seize the palace,[31] do with hands take hold
Of doors, of locks, or bolts; yea, I am bold,
When in, to clamber up unto the throne,
And to possess it, as if 'twere mine own.
Nor is there any law forbidding me
Here to abide, or in this palace be.
Yea, if I please, I do the highest stories
Ascend, there sit, and so behold the glories
Myself is compassed with, as if I were
One of the chiefest courtiers that be there.
Here lords and ladies do come round about me,
With grave demeanour, nor do any flout me
For this, my brave adventure, no, not they;
They come, they go, but leave me there to stay.
Now, my reproacher, I do by all this
Show how thou may'st possess thyself of bliss:
Thou art worse than a spider, but take hold

On Christ the door, thou shalt not be controll'd.
By him do thou the heavenly palace enter;
None chide thee will for this thy brave adventure;
Approach thou then unto the very throne,
There speak thy mind, fear not, the day's thine own;
Nor saint, nor angel, will thee stop or stay,
But rather tumble blocks out of the way.
My venom stops not me; let not thy vice
Stop thee; possess thyself of paradise.
Go on, I say, although thou be a sinner,
Learn to be bold in faith, of me a spinner.
This is the way the glories to possess,
And to enjoy what no man can express.
Sometimes I find the palace door uplock'd,
And so my entrance thither has upblock'd.
But am I daunted? No, I here and there
Do feel and search; so if I anywhere,
At any chink or crevice, find my way,
I crowd, I press for passage, make no stay.
And so through difficulty I attain
The palace; yea, the throne where princes reign.
I crowd sometimes, as if I'd burst in sunder;
And art thou crushed with striving, do not wonder.
Some scarce get in, and yet indeed they enter;
Knock, for they nothing have, that nothing venture.
Nor will the King himself throw dirt on thee,
As thou hast cast reproaches upon me.
He will not hate thee, O thou foul backslider!
As thou didst me, because I am a spider.
Now, to conclude since I such doctrine bring,
Slight me no more, call me not ugly thing.
God wisdom hath unto the piss-ant given,
And spiders may teach men the way to heaven.

Sinner.
Well, my good spider, I my errors see,
I was a fool for railing upon thee.
Thy nature, venom, and thy fearful hue,
Both show that sinners are, and what they do.
Thy way and works do also darkly tell,
How some men go to heaven, and some to hell.
Thou art my monitor, I am a fool;
They learn may, that to spiders go to school.

XIX

MEDITATIONS UPON THE DAY BEFORE THE SUN-RISING

But all this while, where's he whose golden rays
Drives night away and beautifies our days?

Where's he whose goodly face doth warm and heal,
And show us what the darksome nights conceal?
Where's he that thaws our ice, drives cold away?
Let's have him, or we care not for the day.
Thus 'tis with who partakers are of grace,
There's nought to them like their Redeemer's face.

XX

OF THE MOLE IN THE GROUND

The mole's a creature very smooth and slick,
She digs i' th' dirt, but 'twill not on her stick;
So's he who counts this world his greatest gains,
Yet nothing gets but's labour for his pains.
Earth's the mole's element, she can't abide
To be above ground, dirt heaps are her pride;
And he is like her who the worldling plays,
He imitates her in her work and ways.
Poor silly mole, that thou should'st love to be
Where thou nor sun, nor moon, nor stars can see.
But O! how silly's he who doth not care
So he gets earth, to have of heaven a share!

XXI

OF THE CUCKOO

Thou booby, say'st thou nothing but Cuckoo?
The robin and the wren can thee outdo.
They to us play through their little throats,
Taking not one, but sundry pretty taking notes.
But thou hast fellows, some like thee can do
Little but suck our eggs, and sing Cuckoo.
Thy notes do not first welcome in our spring,
Nor dost thou its first tokens to us bring.
Birds less than thee by far, like prophets, do
Tell us, 'tis coming, though not by Cuckoo.
Nor dost thou summer have away with thee,
Though thou a yawling bawling Cuckoo be.
When thou dost cease among us to appear,
Then doth our harvest bravely crown our year.
But thou hast fellows, some like thee can do
Little but suck our eggs, and sing Cuckoo.
Since Cuckoos forward not our early spring,
Nor help with notes to bring our harvest in;
And since, while here, she only makes a noise,
So pleasing unto none as girls and boys,
The Formalist we may compare her to,

For he doth suck our eggs, and sing Cuckoo.

XXII

OF THE BOY AND BUTTERFLY

Behold how eager this our little boy
Is for this Butterfly, as if all joy,
All profits, honours, yea, and lasting pleasures,
Were wrapt up in her, or the richest treasures,
Found in her, would be bundled up together,
When all her all is lighter than a feather.
He halloos, runs, and cries out, Here, boys, here,
Nor doth he brambles or the nettles fear.
He stumbles at the mole-hills, up he gets,
And runs again, as one bereft of wits;
And all this labour and this large outcry,
Is only for a silly butterfly.

Comparison.

This little boy an emblem is of those
Whose hearts are wholly at the world's dispose,
The butterfly doth represent to me,
The world's best things at best but fading be.
All are but painted nothings and false joys,
Like this poor butterfly to these our boys.
His running through nettles, thorns, and briars,
To gratify his boyish fond desires;
His tumbling over mole-hills to attain
His end, namely, his butterfly to gain;
Doth plainly show what hazards some men run.
To get what will be lost as soon as won.
Men seem in choice, than children far more wise,
Because they run not after butterflies;
When yet, alas! for what are empty toys,
They follow children, like to beardless boys.[32]

XXIII

OF THE FLY AT THE CANDLE

What ails this fly thus desperately to enter
A combat with the candle? Will she venture
To clash at light? Away, thou silly fly;
Thus doing thou wilt burn thy wings and die.
But 'tis a folly her advice to give,
She'll kill the candle, or she will not live.
Slap, says she, at it; then she makes retreat,

So wheels about, and doth her blows repeat.
Nor doth the candle let her quite escape,
But gives some little check unto the ape:
Throws up her heels it doth, so down she falls,
Where she lies sprawling, and for succour calls.
When she recovers, up she gets again,
And at the candle comes with might and main,
But now behold, the candle takes the fly,
And holds her, till she doth by burning die.

Comparison.

This candle is an emblem of that light
Our gospel gives in this our darksome night.
The fly a lively picture is of those
That hate and do this gospel light oppose.
At last the gospel doth become their snare,
Doth them with burning hands in pieces tear.[33]

XXIV

ON THE RISING OF THE SUN

Look, look, brave Sol doth peep up from beneath,
Shows us his golden face, doth on us breathe;
He also doth compass us round with glories,
Whilst he ascends up to his highest stories.
Where he his banner over us displays,
And gives us light to see our works and ways.
Nor are we now, as at the peep of light,
To question, is it day, or is it night?
The night is gone, the shadows fled away,
And we now most sure are that it is day.
Our eyes behold it, and our hearts believe it;
Nor can the wit of man in this deceive it.
And thus it is when Jesus shows his face,
And doth assure us of his love and grace.

XXV

UPON THE PROMISING FRUITFULNESS OF A TREE

A comely sight indeed it is to see
A world of blossoms on an apple-tree:
Yet far more comely would this tree appear,
If all its dainty blooms young apples were.
But how much more might one upon it see,
If all would hang there till they ripe should be.
But most of all in beauty 'twould abound,

If then none worm-eaten should there be found.
But we, alas! do commonly behold
Blooms fall apace, if mornings be but cold.
They too, which hang till they young apples are,
By blasting winds and vermin take despair,
Store that do hang, while almost ripe, we see
By blust'ring winds are shaken from the tree,
So that of many, only some there be,
That grow till they come to maturity.

Comparison.

This tree a perfect emblem is of those
Which God doth plant, which in his garden grows,
Its blasted blooms are motions unto good,
Which chill affections do nip in the bud.
Those little apples which yet blasted are,
Show some good purposes, no good fruits bear.
Those spoiled by vermin are to let us see,
How good attempts by bad thoughts ruin'd be.
Those which the wind blows down, while they are green,
Show good works have by trials spoiled been.
Those that abide, while ripe upon the tree,
Show, in a good man, some ripe fruit will be.
Behold then how abortive some fruits are,
Which at the first most promising appear.
The frost, the wind, the worm, with time doth show,
There flows, from much appearance, works but few.

XXVI

UPON THE THIEF

The thief, when he doth steal, thinks he doth gain;
Yet then the greatest loss he doth sustain.
Come, thief, tell me thy gains, but do not falter.
When summ'd, what comes it to more than the halter?
Perhaps, thou'lt say, The halter I defy;
So thou may'st say, yet by the halter die.
Thou'lt say, Then there's an end; no, pr'ythee, hold,
He was no friend of thine that thee so told.
Hear thou the Word of God, that will thee tell,
Without repentance thieves must go to hell.
But should it be as thy false prophet says,
Yet nought but loss doth come by thievish ways.
All honest men will flee thy company,
Thou liv'st a rogue, and so a rogue will die.
Innocent boldness thou hast none at all,
Thy inward thoughts do thee a villain call.
Sometimes when thou liest warmly on thy bed,

Thou art like one unto the gallows led.
Fear, as a constable, breaks in upon thee,
Thou art as if the town was up to stone thee.
If hogs do grunt, or silly rats do rustle,
Thou art in consternation, think'st a bustle
By men about the door, is made to take thee,
And all because good conscience doth forsake thee.
Thy case is most deplorably so bad,
Thou shunn'st to think on't, lest thou should'st be mad.
Thou art beset with mischiefs every way,
The gallows groaneth for thee every day.
Wherefore, I pr'ythee, thief, thy theft forbear,
Consult thy safety, pr'ythee, have a care.
If once thy head be got within the noose,
'Twill be too late a longer life to choose.
As to the penitent thou readest of,
What's that to them who at repentance scoff.
Nor is that grace at thy command or power,
That thou should'st put it off till the last hour.
I pr'ythee, thief, think on't, and turn betime;
Few go to life who do the gallows climb.

XXVII

OF THE CHILD WITH THE BIRD AT THE BUSH

My little bird, how canst thou sit
    And sing amidst so many thorns?
Let me a hold upon thee get,
    My love with honour thee adorns.
Thou art at present little worth,
    Five farthings none will give for thee,
But pr'ythee, little bird, come forth,
    Thou of more value art to me.
'Tis true it is sunshine to-day,
    To-morrow birds will have a storm;
My pretty one come thou away,
    My bosom then shall keep thee warm.
Thou subject are to cold o'nights,
    When darkness is thy covering;
At days thy danger's great by kites,
    How can'st thou then sit there and sing?
Thy food is scarce and scanty too,
    'Tis worms and trash which thou dost eat;
Thy present state I pity do,
    Come, I'll provide thee better meat.
I'll feed thee with white bread and milk,
    And sugar plums, if them thou crave.
I'll cover thee with finest silk,
    That from the cold I may thee save.

My father's palace shall be thine,
   Yea, in it thou shalt sit and sing;
My little bird, if thou'lt be mine,
   The whole year round shall be thy spring.
I'll teach thee all the notes at court,
   Unthought-of music thou shalt play;
And all that thither do resort,
   Shall praise thee for it every day.
I'll keep thee safe from cat and cur,
   No manner o' harm shall come to thee;
Yea, I will be thy succourer,
   My bosom shall thy cabin be.
But lo, behold, the bird is gone;
   These charmings would not make her yield;
The child's left at the bush alone,
   The bird flies yonder o'er the field.

Comparison.

This child of Christ an emblem is,
   The bird to sinners I compare,
The thorns are like those sins of his
   Which do surround him everywhere.
Her songs, her food, and sunshine day,
   Are emblems of those foolish toys,
Which to destruction lead the way,
   The fruit of worldly, empty joys.
The arguments this child doth choose
   To draw to him a bird thus wild,
Shows Christ familiar speech doth use
   To make's to him be reconciled.
The bird in that she takes her wing,
   To speed her from him after all,
Shows us vain man loves any thing
   Much better than the heavenly call.

XXVIII

OF MOSES AND HIS WIFE

This Moses was a fair and comely man,
His wife a swarthy Ethiopian;
Nor did his milk-white bosom change her sin.
She came out thence as black as she went in.
Now Moses was a type of Moses' law,
His wife likewise of one that never saw
Another way unto eternal life;
There's mystery, then, in Moses and his wife.
The law is very holy, just, and good,
And to it is espoused all flesh and blood;

But this its goodness it cannot bestow
On any that are wedded thereunto.
Therefore as Moses' wife came swarthy in,
And went out from him without change of skin,
So he that doth the law for life adore,
Shall yet by it be left a black-a-more.

OF THE ROSE-BUSH

This homely bush doth to mine eyes expose
A very fair, yea, comely ruddy rose.
This rose doth also bow its head to me,
Saying, Come, pluck me, I thy rose will be;
Yet offer I to gather rose or bud,
Ten to one but the bush will have my blood.
This looks like a trapan,[34] or a decoy,
To offer, and yet snap, who would enjoy;
Yea, the more eager on't, the more in danger,
Be he the master of it, or a stranger.
Bush, why dost bear a rose if none must have it.
Who dost expose it, yet claw those that crave it?
Art become freakish? dost the wanton play,
Or doth thy testy humour tend its way?

Comparison.

This rose God's Son is, with his ruddy looks.
But what's the bush, whose pricks, like tenter-hooks,
Do scratch and claw the finest lady's hands,
Or rend her clothes, if she too near it stands?
This bush an emblem is of Adam's race,
Of which Christ came, when he his Father's grace
Commended to us in his crimson blood,
While he in sinners' stead and nature stood.
Thus Adam's race did bear this dainty rose,
And doth the same to Adam's race expose;
But those of Adam's race which at it catch,
Adam's race will them prick, and claw, and scratch.

XXX

OF THE GOING DOWN OF THE SUN

What, hast thou run thy race, art going down?
Thou seemest angry, why dost on us frown?
Yea, wrap thy head with clouds and hide thy face,
As threatening to withdraw from us thy grace?

O leave us not! When once thou hid'st thy head,
Our horizon with darkness will be spread.
Tell who hath thee offended, turn again.
Alas! too late, intreaties are in vain.

Comparison.

Our gospel has had here a summer's day,
But in its sunshine we, like fools, did play;
Or else fall out, and with each other wrangle,
And did, instead of work, not much but jangle.
And if our sun seems angry, hides his face,
Shall it go down, shall night possess this place?
Let not the voice of night birds us afflict,
And of our misspent summer us convict.[35]

XXXI

UPON THE FROG

The frog by nature is both damp and cold,
Her mouth is large, her belly much will hold;
She sits somewhat ascending, loves to be
Croaking in gardens, though unpleasantly.

Comparison.

The hypocrite is like unto this frog,
As like as is the puppy to the dog.
He is of nature cold, his mouth is wide
To prate, and at true goodness to deride.
He mounts his head as if he was above
The world, when yet 'tis that which has his love.
And though he seeks in churches for to croak,
He neither loveth Jesus nor his yoke.

XXXII

UPON THE WHIPPING OF A TOP

'Tis with the whip the boy sets up the top,
   The whip makes it run round upon its toe;
The whip makes it hither and thither hop:
   'Tis with the whip the top is made to go.

Comparison.

Our legalist is like unto this top,
   Without a whip he doth not duty do;

Let Moses whip him, he will skip and hop;
   Forbear to whip, he'll neither stand nor go.

XXXIII

UPON THE PISMIRE

Must we unto the pismire go to school,
   To learn of her in summer to provide
For winter next ensuing. Man's a fool,
   Or silly ants would not be made his guide.
But, sluggard, is it not a shame for thee
   To be outdone by pismires? Pr'ythee hear:
Their works, too, will thy condemnation be
   When at the judgment-seat thou shalt appear.
But since thy God doth bid thee to her go,
   Obey, her ways consider, and be wise;
The piss-ant tell thee will what thou must do,
   And set the way to life before thine eyes.

XXXIV

UPON THE BEGGAR

He wants, he asks, he pleads his poverty,
They within doors do him an alms deny.
He doth repeat and aggravate his grief,
But they repulse him, give him no relief.
He begs, they say, Begone; he will not hear,
But coughs, sighs, and makes signs he still is there;
They disregard him, he repeats his groans;
They still say nay, and he himself bemoans.
They grow more rugged, they call him vagrant;
He cries the shriller, trumpets out his want.
At last, when they perceive he'll take no nay,
An alms they give him without more delay.

Comparison.

This beggar doth resemble them that pray
To God for mercy, and will take no nay,
But wait, and count that all his hard gainsays
Are nothing else but fatherly delays;
Then imitate him, praying souls, and cry:
There's nothing like to importunity.

XXXV

UPON THE HORSE AND HIS RIDER

There's one rides very sagely on the road,
Showing that he affects the gravest mode.
Another rides tantivy, or full trot,
To show much gravity he matters not.
Lo, here comes one amain, he rides full speed,
Hedge, ditch, nor miry bog, he doth not heed.
One claws it up-hill without stop or check,
Another down as if he'd break his neck.
Now every horse has his especial guider;
Then by his going you may know the rider.

Comparison.

Now let us turn our horse into a man,
His rider to a spirit, if we can.
Then let us, by the methods of the guider,
Tell every horse how he should know his rider.
Some go, as men, direct in a right way,
Nor are they suffered to go astray;
As with a bridle they are governed,
And kept from paths which lead unto the dead.
Now this good man has his especial guider,
Then by his going let him know his rider.
Some go as if they did not greatly care,
Whether of heaven or hell they should be heir.
The rein, it seems, is laid upon their neck,
They seem to go their way without a check.
Now this man too has his especial guider,
And by his going he may know his rider.
Some again run as if resolved to die,
Body and soul, to all eternity.
Good counsel they by no means can abide;
They'll have their course whatever them betide.
Now these poor men have their especial guider,
Were they not fools they soon might know their rider.
There's one makes head against all godliness,
Those too, that do profess it, he'll distress;
He'll taunt and flout if goodness doth appear,
And at its countenancers mock and jeer.
Now this man, too, has his especial guider,
And by his going he might know his rider.

XXXVI

UPON THE SIGHT OF A POUND OF CANDLES FALLING TO THE GROUND

But be the candles down, and scattered too,
Some lying here, some there? What shall we do?

Hold, light the candle there that stands on high,
It you may find the other candles by.
Light that, I say, and so take up the pound
You did let fall and scatter on the ground.

Comparison.

The fallen candles do us intimate
The bulk of God's elect in their laps'd state;
Their lying scattered in the dark may be
To show, by man's lapsed state, his misery.
The candle that was taken down and lighted,
Thereby to find them fallen and benighted,
Is Jesus Christ; God, by his light, doth gather
Who he will save, and be unto a Father.

XXXVII

UPON A PENNY LOAF

Thy price one penny is in time of plenty,
In famine doubled, 'tis from one to twenty.
Yea, no man knows what price on thee to set
When there is but one penny loaf to get.

Comparison.

This loaf's an emblem of the Word of God,
A thing of low esteem before the rod
Of famine smites the soul with fear of death,
But then it is our all, our life, our breath.[36]

XXXVIII

THE BOY AND WATCHMAKER

This watch my father did on me bestow,
A golden one it is, but 'twill not go,
Unless it be at an uncertainty:
But as good none as one to tell a lie.
When 'tis high day my hand will stand at nine;
I think there's no man's watch so bad as mine.
Sometimes 'tis sullen, 'twill not go at all,
And yet 'twas never broke nor had a fall.

Watchmaker.

Your watch, though it be good, through want of skill
May fail to do according to your will.

Suppose the balance, wheels, and springs be good,
And all things else, unless you understood
To manage it, as watches ought to be,
Your watch will still be at uncertainty.
Come, tell me, do you keep it from the dust,
Yea, wind it also duly up you must?
Take heed, too, that you do not strain the spring;
You must be circumspect in every thing,
Or else your watch, were it as good again,
Would not with time and tide you entertain.

Comparison.

This boy an emblem is of a convert,
His watch of the work of grace within his heart,
The watchmaker is Jesus Christ our Lord,
His counsel, the directions of his Word;
Then convert, if thy heart be out of frame,
Of this watchmaker learn to mend the same.
Do not lay ope' thy heart to worldly dust,
Nor let thy graces over-grow with rust,
Be oft' renewed in the' spirit of thy mind,
Or else uncertain thou thy watch wilt find.

XXXIX

UPON A LOOKING-GLASS

In this see thou thy beauty, hast thou any,
Or thy defects, should they be few or many.
Thou may'st, too, here thy spots and freckles see,
Hast thou but eyes, and what their numbers be.
But art thou blind? There is no looking-glass
Can show thee thy defects, thy spots, or face.

Comparison.

Unto this glass we may compare the Word,
For that to man advantage doth afford
(Has he a mind to know himself and state),
To see what will be his eternal fate.
But without eyes, alas! how can he see?
Many that seem to look here, blind men be.
This is the reason they so often read
Their judgment there, and do it nothing dread.

XL

OF THE LOVE OF CHRIST

The love of Christ, poor I! may touch upon;
But 'tis unsearchable. O! there is none
Its large dimensions can comprehend
Should they dilate thereon world without end.
When we had sinned, in his zeal he sware,
That he upon his back our sins would bear.
And since unto sin is entailed death,
He vowed for our sins he'd lose his breath.
He did not only say, vow, or resolve,
But to astonishment did so involve
Himself in man's distress and misery,
As for, and with him, both to live and die.
To his eternal fame in sacred story,
We find that he did lay aside his glory,
Stepped from the throne of highest dignity,
Became poor man, did in a manger lie;
Yea, was beholden unto his for bread,
Had, of his own, not where to lay his head;
Though rich, he did for us become thus poor,
That he might make us rich for evermore.
Nor was this but the least of what he did,
But the outside of what he suffered?
God made his blessed son under the law,
Under the curse, which, like the lion's paw,
Did rent and tear his soul for mankind's sin,
More than if we for it in hell had been.
His cries, his tears, and bloody agony,
The nature of his death doth testify.
Nor did he of constraint himself thus give,
For sin, to death, that man might with him live.
He did do what he did most willingly,
He sung, and gave God thanks, that he must die.
But do kings use to die for captive slaves?
Yet we were such when Jesus died to save's.
Yea, when he made himself a sacrifice,
It was that he might save his enemies.
And though he was provoked to retract
His blest resolves for such so good an act,
By the abusive carriages of those
That did both him, his love, and grace oppose;
Yet he, as unconcerned with such things,
Goes on, determines to make captives kings;
Yea, many of his murderers he takes
Into his favour, and them princes makes.

XLI

ON THE CACKLING OF A HEN

The hen, so soon as she an egg doth lay,
(Spreads the fame of her doing what she may.)
About the yard she cackling now doth go,
To tell what 'twas she at her nest did do.
Just thus it is with some professing men,
If they do ought that good is, like our hen
They can but cackle on't where e'er they go,
What their right hand doth their left hand must know.

XLII

UPON AN HOUR-GLASS

This glass, when made, was, by the workman's skill,
The sum of sixty minutes to fulfil.
Time, more nor less, by it will out be spun,
But just an hour, and then the glass is run.
Man's life we will compare unto this glass,
The number of his months he cannot pass;
But when he has accomplished his day,
He, like a vapour, vanisheth away.

XLIII

UPON A SNAIL

She goes but softly, but she goeth sure,
    She stumbles not, as stronger creatures do.
Her journey's shorter, so she may endure
    Better than they which do much farther go.
She makes no noise, but stilly seizeth on
    The flower or herb appointed for her food,
The which she quietly doth feed upon
    While others range and glare, but find no good.
And though she doth but very softly go,
    However, 'tis not fast nor slow, but sure;
And certainly they that do travel so,
    The prize they do aim at they do procure.

Comparison.

Although they seem not much to stir, less go,
    For Christ that hunger, or from wrath that flee,
Yet what they seek for quickly they come to,
    Though it doth seem the farthest off to be.
One act of faith doth bring them to that flower
    They so long for, that they may eat and live,
Which, to attain, is not in others power,
    Though for it a king's ransom they would give.

Then let none faint, nor be at all dismayed
   That life by Christ do seek, they shall not fail
To have it; let them nothing be afraid;
   The herb and flower are eaten by the snail.[37]

XLIV

OF THE SPOUSE OF CHRIST

Who's this that cometh from the wilderness,
   Like smokey pillars thus perfum'd with myrrh,
Leaning upon her dearest in distress,
   Led into's bosom by the Comforter?
She's clothed with the sun, crowned with twelve stars,
   The spotted moon her footstool she hath made.
The dragon her assaults, fills her with jars,
   Yet rests she under her Beloved's shade,
But whence was she? what is her pedigree?
   Was not her father a poor Amorite?
What was her mother but as others be,
   A poor, a wretched, and a sinful Hittite.
Yea, as for her, the day that she was born,
   As loathsome, out of doors they did her cast;
Naked and filthy, stinking and forlorn;
   This was her pedigree from first to last.
Nor was she pitied in this estate,
   All let her lie polluted in her blood:
None her condition did commiserate,
   There was no heart that sought to do her good.
Yet she unto these ornaments is come,
   Her breasts are fashioned, her hair is grown;
She is made heiress of the best kingdom;
   All her indignities away are blown.
Cast out she was, but now she home is taken,
   Naked (sometimes), but now, you see, she's cloth'd;
Now made the darling, though before forsaken,
   Barefoot, but now as princes' daughters shod.
Instead of filth, she now has her perfumes;
   Instead of ignominy, her chains of gold:
Instead of what the beauty most consumes,
   Her beauty's perfect, lovely to behold.
Those that attend and wait upon her be
   Princes of honour, clothed in white array;
Upon her head's a crown of gold, and she
   Eats wheat, honey, and oil, from day to day.
For her beloved, he's the high'st of all,
   The only Potentate, the King of kings:
Angels and men do him Jehovah call,
   And from him life and glory always springs.
He's white and ruddy, and of all the chief:

His head, his locks, his eyes, his hands, and feet,
  Do, for completeness, out-go all belief;
  His cheeks like flowers are, his mouth most sweet.
As for his wealth, he is made heir of all;
  What is in heaven, what is on earth is his:
And he this lady his joint-heir doth call,
  Of all that shall be, or at present is.
Well, lady, well, God has been good to thee;
  Thou of an outcast, now art made a queen.
Few, or none, may with thee compared be,
  A beggar made thus high is seldom seen.
Take heed of pride, remember what thou art
  By nature, though thou hast in grace a share,
Thou in thyself dost yet retain a part
  Of thine own filthiness; wherefore beware.

XLV

UPON A SKILFUL PLAYER OF AN INSTRUMENT

He that can play well on an instrument,
  Will take the ear, and captivate the mind
With mirth or sadness; for that it is bent
  Thereto, as music in it place doth find.
But if one hears that hath therein no skill,
  (As often music lights of such a chance)
Of its brave notes they soon be weary will:
  And there are some can neither sing nor dance.

Comparison.

Unto him that thus skilfully doth play,
  God doth compare a gospel-minister,
That rightly preacheth, and doth godly pray,
  Applying truly what doth thence infer.
This man, whether of wrath or grace he preach,
  So skilfully doth handle every word;
And by his saying doth the heart so reach,
  That it doth joy or sigh before the Lord.
But some there be, which, as the brute, doth lie
  Under the Word, without the least advance
Godward; such do despise the ministry;
  They weep not at it, neither to it dance.

XLVI

OF MAN BY NATURE

From God he's a backslider,

Of ways he loves the wider;
With wickedness a sider,
More venom than a spider.
In sin he's a considerer,
A make-bate and divider;
Blind reason is his guider,
The devil is his rider.

UPON THE DISOBEDIENT CHILD

Children become, while little, our delights!
When they grow bigger, they begin to fright's.
Their sinful nature prompts them to rebel,
And to delight in paths that lead to hell.
Their parents' love and care they overlook,
As if relation had them quite forsook.
They take the counsels of the wanton's, rather
Than the most grave instructions of a father.
They reckon parents ought to do for them,
Though they the fifth commandment do contemn;
They snap and snarl if parents them control,
Though but in things most hurtful to the soul.
They reckon they are masters, and that we
Who parents are, should to them subject be!
If parents fain would have a hand in choosing,
The children have a heart will in refusing.
They'll by wrong doings, under parents gather,
And say it is no sin to rob a father.
They'll jostle parents out of place and power,
They'll make themselves the head, and them devour.
How many children, by becoming head,
Have brought their parents to a piece of bread!
Thus they who, at the first, were parents joy,
Turn that to bitterness, themselves destroy.

But, wretched child, how canst thou thus requite
Thy aged parents, for that great delight
They took in thee, when thou, as helpless, lay
In their indulgent bosoms day by day?
Thy mother, long before she brought thee forth,
Took care thou shouldst want neither food nor cloth.
Thy father glad was at his very heart,
Had he to thee a portion to impart.
Comfort they promised themselves in thee,
But thou, it seems, to them a grief wilt be.
How oft, how willingly brake they their sleep,
If thou, their bantling, didst but winch or weep.
Their love to thee was such they could have giv'n,

That thou mightst live, almost their part of heav'n.
But now, behold how they rewarded are!
For their indulgent love and tender care;
All is forgot, this love he doth despise.
They brought this bird up to pick out their eyes.

UPON A SHEET OF WHITE PAPER

This subject is unto the foulest pen,
Or fairest handled by the sons of men.
'Twill also show what is upon it writ,
Be it wisely, or nonsense for want of wit,
Each blot and blur it also will expose
To thy next readers, be they friends or foes.

Comparison.

Some souls are like unto this blank or sheet,
Though not in whiteness. The next man they meet,
If wise or fool, debauched or deluder,
Or what you will, the dangerous intruder
May write thereon, to cause that man to err
In doctrine or in life, with blot and blur.
Nor will that soul conceal from who observes,
But show how foul it is, wherein it swerves.
A reading man may know who was the writer,
And, by the hellish nonsense, the inditer.

XLIX

UPON FIRE

Who falls into the fire shall burn with heat;
While those remote scorn from it to retreat.
Yea, while those in it, cry out, O! I burn,
Some farther off those cries to laughter turn.

Comparison.

While some tormented are in hell for sin;
On earth some greatly do delight therein.
Yea, while some make it echo with their cry,
Others count it a fable and a lie.[38]

FOOTNOTES:

[1] Bunyan's poem in the Holy War.

[2] On the leaf following the title to One Thing is Needful, &c., by John Bunyan, 1688. A rare little 32mo, published by the author, in possession of the Editor.

[3] At the end of Grace Abounding, the sixth edition, and also in The Work of Jesus Christ as an Advocate, by Bunyan, 1688.

[4] Advertised in the eighth edition of Solomon's Temple Spiritualized.

[5] In Youth Directed and Instructed–a curious little book for children.

[6] Square 24mo., by Bennet, Gurney, and others, without date.

[7] Sturt engraved the Book of Common Prayer; some French artists elegantly etched two of their devotional books; and Pyne engraved the texts of Horace and Virgil with beautiful vignettes.

[8] Altered to 'huge' in the Emblems, 1724.

[9] A familiar phrase, denoting persons who have been always frivolous and childish, or those who have passed into second childhood. 'On the shelf' is a common saying of ladies when they are too old to get married.–Ed.

[10] The name of a bird that mimics gestures.–Ed.

[11] Indelible, as when raw material is dyed before it is wove, every grain receives the dye.–Ed.

[12] For this use of the word 'handle,' see Jeremiah 2:8. 'They that handle the law.'–Ed.

[13] This word, with pismire and emmet, has become obsolete. 'Ant' is the term now universally used.–Ed.

[14] See Psalm 84:3; Leviticus 11:16; Numbers 20.

[15] A machine used in the manufacture of cloth, on which it is stretched.–Ed.

[16] Spiders being venomous was a vulgar error, universally believed, until modern discoveries have proved the contrary, excepting a few foreign species.–Ed.

[17] This is a scriptural idea of the inhabitants of heaven. Revelation 11:8, saints 'small and great.' Matthew 19:28: 'The Son of man on his throne, and the twelve apostles on their thrones.' Revelation 4:10: 'Four and twenty elders on their thrones.' Revelation 5:11: 'An innumerable company of worshippers.'–Ed.

[18] In an ancient battledore or horn-book, and in one of Henry VIII's primers, both in the editor's possession, this sentence is translated–'And let us not be led into temptation.'–Ed.

[19] When divine light first dawns upon the soul, and reveals sin, O how difficult is it to conclude that sin is pardoned, and the sinner blest!–Ed.

[20] The swallow is remarkably swift in flight; 'their note is a slight twittering, which they seldom if ever exert but upon the wing.'–Goldsmith's Natural History.–Ed.

[21] 'Be in print'; a proverbial expression, to show order and regularity; like type in print.–Ed.

[22] 'Ley'; barren or fallow, uncultivated, generally spelt lea.–Ed.

[23] This riddle is solved in the fourth line following. The light of the fear and love of God begins in the middle of our bodily frame, with the heart. Bunyan's love of religious riddles is seen in the second part of the Pilgrimage, when Christian is resting at the house of Gaius.–Ed.

[24] Convictions of sin make the soul turn from sin.–Ed.

[25] This character is admirably drawn in the second part of the Pilgrim's Progress–Mr. Brisk, a suitor to Mercy.–Ed.

[26] Preterite of the verb 'to save,' from the Saxon agan, to be held or bound by moral obligation.–Imperial Dictionary.–Ed.

[27] What folly, nay, madness, for man to pretend to make God of a little flour, or to rely for forgiveness of sin on a wafer, a bit of bread, or a little wine or water. How degraded is he that pretends to believe such palpable absurdities.–Ed.

[28] This is one of Bunyan's keen, shrewd, home thrusts. Clothes professedly made to hide what they studiously display!!–Ed.

[29] Possessed me with, or has given me possession of.–Ed.

[30] Man's sinfulness, by nature and practice, justly, but awfully described.–Mason.

[31] See Proverbs 30:20, and Pilgrim's Progress. There is also a very striking allusion to the subject of this emblem, in Bunyan's Light in Darkness.

[32] He who, in riper years, seeks happiness in sensual gratification, is a child in understanding: he only changes his toys.–Ed.

[33] 'To the one, a savour of death unto death; and to the other, a savour of life unto life' (2 Cor 2:16).

[34] 'Trapan' is the Saxon verb to ensnare, modernized to trap.–Ed.

[35] How agonizing will be the cry of the lost soul–'The harvest is past, the summer is ended, and we are not saved' (Jer 8:20).–Ed. Upon the brittle thread of life hang everlasting things.–Mason.

[36] When the Word of God dwells in us richly in all wisdom, then will the peace of God rule in our hearts, and we shall be sweetly inclined to every good thought, word, and work.–Ed.

[37] If the crawling snail finds food, wherefore do ye doubt, O! ye of little faith.–Ed.

[38] Fools make a mock at sin. The scorner occupies a proud, an elevated seat, which will sink under him, and crush him down to everlasting destruction. The threatenings and promises of God stand sure for ever.–Ed

John Bunyan – A Short Biography

John Bunyan was born appropriately enough at Bunyan's End in the parish of Elstow, near Bedford to Thomas and Margaret Bunyan. The exact date is unknown he was, however, baptized on November 30th, 1628.

By his own account, Bunyan in his youth enjoyed bell-ringing, dancing and playing games unfortunately sometimes on the Sunday Sabbath, these pleasures were to be later outlawed by the Puritan regime under Cromwell.

As a child Bunyan learned his father's trade of tinker (a mender of pots and pans) and was given some basic schooling. In his autobiographical work, Grace Abounding to the Chief of Sinners, Bunyan recorded little of his upbringing, but he did note how he picked up the habit of swearing from his father, suffered from nightmares, and read the popular stories of the day in cheap chap-books.

In the summer of 1644, shortly before his 16th birthday, Bunyan lost both his mother and his sister Margaret.

That autumn, Bunyan enlisted in the Parliamentary army after 225 recruits from the town of Bedford were demanded to fight in the Civil War. A muster roll for the garrison of Newport Pagnell shows him as private "John Bunnian". In Grace Abounding to the Chief of Sinners, he recounted an incident from this time, as evidence of the grace of God:

"When I was a Souldier I, with others were drawn out to go to such a place to besiege it; But when I was just ready to go, one of the company desired to go in my room, to which, when I had consented, he took my place; and coming to the siege, as he stood Sentinel, he was shot into the head with a Musket bullet and died."

Bunyan's army service provided him with a knowledge of military language which he used in his book The Holy War. These army years also exposed him to the ideas of the various religious sects and radical groups. The garrison town of Newport Pagnell also gave him opportunities to indulge in behaviour he would later confess to in Grace Abounding to the Chief of Sinners: "So that until I came to the state of Marriage, I was the very ringleader of all the Youth that kept me company, in all manner of vice and ungodliness".

Bunyan spent nearly three years in the army, leaving in 1647 to return to Elstow and a trade as a tinker.

Within two years of leaving service Bunyan married. The name of his wife and the date of his marriage are not recorded but Bunyan did write that his wife, a pious young woman, brought with her into the marriage two books that she had inherited from her father: Arthur Dent's Plain Man's Pathway to Heaven and Lewis Bayly's Practice of Piety. He claimed also that, apart from the books, the newly-weds possessed little: "not having so much household-stuff as a Dish or a Spoon betwixt us both".

The couple's first daughter, Mary, was born in 1650, and it soon became apparent that she was blind. They would have three more children, Elizabeth, Thomas and John.

It was only after his marriage that he developed a deeper interest in religion, attending, at first, the local parish church and then joining the Bedford Meeting, a non-conformist group in Bedford, where he became a preacher.

The story that has gained credence is that one Sunday the vicar of Elstow preached a sermon against Sabbath breaking, which Bunyan took to heart. One afternoon, as he was playing tip-cat (a game in which a small piece of wood is hit with a bat) on Elstow village green, he heard a voice from the heavens "Wilt thou leave thy sins, and go to Heaven? Or have thy sins, and go to Hell?" These next few years were filled with spiritual conflict as he struggled with doubts and fears over religion and the guilt of what he thought was his own state of sin.

His journey began when Bunyan happened to be in Bedford and passed a group of women talking about spiritual matters. They were founding members of the Bedford Free Church or Meeting and Bunyan, who had been attending the parish church of Elstow, was so impressed by their talk that he joined their church. At that time the non-conformist group was meeting in St John's church in Bedford under the leadership of former Royalist army officer John Gifford. At the instigation of other members of the congregation Bunyan began to preach, both in the church and to groups of people in the surrounding countryside.

In 1656, having by this time moved his family to St Cuthbert's Street in Bedford, he published his first book, Gospel Truths Opened, which was inspired by a dispute with Quakers.

Tragically in 1658 Bunyan's wife died, leaving him with four small children. The following year later he re-married to an eighteen-year-old woman called Elizabeth.

With the death of Cromwell, and with it the end of the Republic Charles II was restored to the throne in 1660. The religious tolerance which had allowed Bunyan the freedom to preach now became curtailed. The members of the Bedford Meeting were no longer able to meet in St John's church, which they had been sharing with the Anglican congregation.

That November, Bunyan was preaching at Lower Samsell, a farm near the village of Westoning, and was told there was a warrant was out for his arrest. Deciding not to effect an escape, he was arrested and brought before the local magistrate, Sir Francis Wingate, at Harlington House.

Under the reign of Charles II religious freedom was, ironically, no longer to be tolerated. Whilst the Act of Uniformity, which made it compulsory for preachers to be ordained by an Anglican bishop and the revised Book of Common Prayer to be used in church services, was still two years away, and the Act of Conventicles, which made it illegal to hold religious meetings of five or more people outside the Church of England was not passed until 1664.

The authorities had arrested Bunyan under the Conventicle Act of 1593, which made it an offence to attend a religious gathering other than at the parish church with more than five people outside their family. This offence was punishable by 3 months imprisonment followed by banishment or execution if the person then failed to promise not to re-offend. The Act had been little used, and Bunyan's arrest was probably due in part to concerns that non-conformist religious meetings were being held as a cover for people plotting against the king although there is no evidence to suggest that was the case with Bunyan's meetings.

His trial took place in January 1661 at the quarter sessions in Bedford, before a group of magistrates under John Kelynge (who would later help to draw up the Act of Uniformity). Bunyan, who had been held in prison since his arrest, was indicted of having "devilishly and perniciousy abstained from coming to church to hear divine service" and having held "several unlawful meetings and conventicles, to the great disturbance and distraction of the good subjects of this kingdom". He was sentenced to three months imprisonment with transportation to follow if at the end of this time he didn't agree to attend the parish church and desist from preaching.

Bunyan refused to agree to give up preaching and his period of imprisonment eventually extended to 12 years in Bedford County Gaol, which stood on the corner of the High Street and Silver Street. His stance caused great hardship to his family, Elizabeth, made many strenuous attempts to obtain his release, and had been pregnant when her husband was arrested and she subsequently gave birth prematurely to a still-born child. She was left to bring up four step-children and to rely on the charity of Bunyan's fellow members of the Bedford Meeting and supporters. Bunyan's only meagre earnings in gaol were from making shoelaces and contributed little to family finances.

Despite their precarious state Bunyan remained resolute: "O I saw in this condition I was a man who was pulling down his house upon the head of his Wife and Children; yet thought I, I must do it, I must do it".

However, on several occasions when he was allowed out of prison, depending on the gaolers or the mood of the authorities at the time, he was even to attend the Bedford Meetings and even preach. His daughter Sarah was born during his imprisonment (the other child of his second marriage, Joseph, was born after his release in 1672).

In prison, Bunyan had a copy of the Bible and of John Foxe's Book of Martyrs, and access to writing materials and the company of other preachers who had been imprisoned. During these dark years he wrote Grace Abounding to the Chief of Sinners and started work on The Pilgrim's Progress, as well as penning several tracts that may have brought him a little extra money. In 1671, while still in prison, he was chosen as pastor of the Bedford Meeting.

By now, with the monarchy allowing increasing religious toleration, the king issued, in March 1672, a declaration of indulgence which suspended penal laws against non-conformists. Thousands were released from prison, amongst them Bunyan shortly after in May. He immediately sought and obtained a licence to preach under the declaration of indulgence and devoted his time to writing and preaching. He continued as pastor of the Bedford Meeting and travelled on horseback to preach, becoming known affectionately as "Bishop Bunyan". His preaching also took him to London, where Lord Mayor Sir John Shorter became a friend and presented him with a silver-mounted walking stick.

The Pilgrim's Progress was published in 1678 by Nathaniel Ponder and was an immediate success and bringing the family some financial comfort. Indeed, Bunyan's later years, in spite of another short term of imprisonment, were spent in relative comfort as a popular author and preacher, and pastor of the Bedford Meeting.

In 1688, on his way to London, Bunyan detoured to Reading, Berkshire, to try and resolve a quarrel. After he continued to London to the house of his friend, the grocer John Strudwick of Snow Hill in the City of London. He was caught in a storm and fell ill with a fever.

John Bunyan died in Strudwick's house on the morning of 31st August, 1688. He was buried in Bunhill Fields non-conformist burial ground in London.

Bunyan's estate at his death was worth £42 19s 0d. His widow Elizabeth died 3 years later in 1691.

The Pilgrim's Progress is one of the most published books in the English language with almost 1,500 editions having been printed.

Between 1656 when he published his first work, Some Gospel Truths Opened, and his death in 1688, Bunyan published 42 titles. A further two works, including his Last Sermon, were published the following year by George Larkin.

In 1692 Southwark comb-maker Charles Doe, who was a friend of Bunyan's later years, brought out, a collection of the author's works, including 12 previously unpublished titles, mostly sermons. Eventually in total the Bunyan canon was 58 titles.

It is the allegory, The Pilgrim's Progress, that made Bunyan's name as an author and for which he is best remembered. During the 18th century Bunyan's rather raw style fell from favour, but his popularity returned with Romanticism, the poet Robert Southey writing an appreciative biography in 1830.

Bunyan's reputation was further enhanced by the evangelical revival and he became a favourite author of the Victorians. The tercentenary of Bunyan's birth, celebrated in 1928, ironically brought praise from his former adversary, the Church of England.

John Bunyan – A Selected Bibliography
Among Bunyan's many works:

A Few Sighs from Hell, or the Groans of a Damned Soul, 1658
A Discourse Upon the Pharisee and the Publican, 1685
A Holy Life
Christ a Complete Saviour (The Intercession of Christ And Who Are Privileged in It), 1692
Come and Welcome to Jesus Christ, 1678
Grace Abounding to the Chief of Sinners, 1666
Light for Them that Sit in Darkness
Praying with the Spirit and with Understanding too, 1663
Of Antichrist and His Ruin, 1692
Reprobation Asserted, 1674
Saved by Grace, 1675
Seasonal Counsel or Suffering Saints in the Furnace – Advice to Persecuted Christians in Their Trials & Tribulations, 1684
Solomon's Temple Spiritualized
Some Gospel Truths Opened, 1656
The Acceptable Sacrifice
The Desire of the Righteous Granted
The Doctrine of the Law and Grace Unfolded, 1659
The Doom and Downfall of the Fruitless Professor (Or The Barren Fig Tree), 1682
The End of the World, The Resurrection of the Dead and Eternal Judgment, 1665
The Fear of God – What it is, and what is it is not, 1679
The Greatness of the Soul and Unspeakableness of its Loss Thereof, 1683
The Heavenly Footman, 1698

The Holy City or the New Jerusalem, 1665
The Holy War – The Losing and Taking Again of the Town of Man-soul (The Holy War Made by Shaddai upon Diabolus, for the Regaining of the World), 1682
The Life and Death of Mr Badman, 1680
The Pilgrim's Progress, 1678
The Strait Gate, Great Difficulty of Going to Heaven, 1676
The Saint's Knowledge of Christ's Love, or The Unsearchable Riches of Christ, 1692
The Water of Life or The Richness and Glory of the Gospel, 1688
The Work of Jesus Christ as an Advocate, 1688

www.ingramcontent.com/pod-product-compliance
Lightning Source LLC
Chambersburg PA
CBHW060134050426
42448CB00010B/2114